GCSE

Business Studies
Revision Guide

Neil Denby

Philip Allan Updates
Market Place
Deddington
Oxfordshire
OX15 0SE

Orders

Bookpoint Ltd, 130 Milton Park, Abingdon, Oxfordshire, OX14 4SB
tel: 01235 827720
fax: 01235 400454
e-mail: uk.orders@bookpoint.co.uk
Lines are open 9.00 a.m.–5.00 p.m., Monday to Saturday, with a 24-hour message answering service. You can also order through the Philip Allan Updates website: www.philipallan.co.uk.

© Philip Allan Updates 2007

ISBN 978-1-84489-438-3

This book has been written specifically to support students studying OCR (A) GCSE Business Studies. The content has been neither approved nor endorsed by OCR and remains the sole responsibility of the author.

All efforts have been made to trace copyright on items used.

All website addresses included in this book are correct at the time of going to press but may subsequently change.

Printed in Great Britain by CPI Bath.

Philip Allan Update's policy is to use papers that are natural, renewable and recyclable products and made from wood grown in sustainable forests. The logging and manufacturing processes are expected to conform to the environmental regulations of the country of origin.

Contents

Introduction

How to revise

Revision is not just about remembering; it is also about being able to apply what you have remembered to business situations. You should make sure that as well as learning the facts, you also understand how a business would use them in its decision making. There are very few questions that will ask you for straightforward knowledge.

Here are ten tips for effective revision:

- Start revising in plenty of time. You may have to revisit some topics at the last minute, but should try to make sure these are very few.
- Have a set time and place for your revision sessions — for example, somewhere you cannot be disturbed.
- Plan revision carefully — make sure that you leave enough time to cover everything.
- Plan short-term targets — 'I will have learnt xxx by xxx'. These help to monitor your progress and to motivate you.
- Don't do too much! Your brain needs regular rests in order to be able to process and store information effectively.
- Revise topics three times. This will help to put the knowledge into your long-term memory.
- Make sure your revision is active — make notes, use spider diagrams, pictograms and mind maps and even try writing raps or song lyrics. Audio and visual reminders are usually better than just words.
- Think about using new technology. You could make a podcast of a revision topic and listen to it on your MP3 player.
- Practise applying your knowledge to business situations. Use the questions in this book to improve your examination technique. Make sure you draw on all the relevant information, not just a single topic.
- Revise with someone else — then you can test each other and compare notes.

How to use this book

This book contains the basic knowledge you need to pass at GCSE. Each chapter is divided into small topics, each of which has a number of features.

- **Core knowledge** outlines the area of knowledge that it is absolutely essential for you to know about each topic.
- **Speak the language** gives the key terms and definitions that you need for that particular topic. In all GCSE business examinations there are marks

for using the correct technical language. The key terms are in **bold** in the text.

- **Boost your grade** gives the types of points or areas of knowledge that you can use to make sure that you earn a better grade.
- **Key points** repeats the main points of knowledge that you need, often in a diagram, table or other visual format.
- **What does the specification require?** gives hints and tips related to what the specification needs you to know, and steers you in the direction of the types of question that can be asked.
- **Test yourself** provides a short test on the content of all or part of the topic. This is in the form of multiple-choice questions, missing word questions or tests that you can self-set.
- **Try this** is linked directly to the specification, asking questions in the style of one of the examination papers. The number of marks given here is an indication of how detailed an answer you should give.

At the end of each chapter, you will find a longer question and a set of multiple-choice questions or similar exercise to test your knowledge. Suggested answers to all the questions and exercises are provided at the end of the book.

Your specification

OCR Specification A is structured so that everyone takes three elements. These consist of either two papers plus coursework, or three examination papers.

The first of the two papers is a **core paper**, which concentrates (as you would expect) on the areas of the specification that have been studied by everyone. These are as follows:

External environment of business
- Business activity
- The organisation
- The changing business environment

Business structure, organisation and control
- Ownership and internal organisation
- Financing business activity

Business behaviour
- Marketing
- Production
- Financial information and decision making

People in organisations
- Human needs and rewards
- Management and recruitment
- Training and staff development

Aiding and controlling business activity
■ Reasons for regulating business activity
■ Influences on business activity

The second paper is the **'option' paper**. While concentrating on the area chosen by the candidate, this may also ask questions based on core material. The options are as follows:

Business and change
■ Economic environment
■ Business environment
■ The business
■ Finance and change

Business communication and marketing
■ Communication in business activity
■ The impact of e-commerce on business activity
■ Marketing and the business environment
■ Marketing: developments and constraints

As well as these two papers, there is a **coursework option** or an **alternative paper to coursework**, which is based on a case study.

Questions in OCR Specification A papers are asked within the context of brief case studies or business scenarios, except in the coursework alternative paper, where questions are based on a pre-seen case study that contains more detail. The case study usually covers a wide range of business terms and concepts, and many of the activities of a business.

Each 'Try this' examination practice question in this book is presented in the style of one of these papers.

There are 20 'Try this' questions in the style of the **core paper**. These are based on two business case studies: Fiveways Farm (see page viii) and Sarah's Hairdressing (see pages viii–ix). Questions on Fiveways are asked in:

■ **Chapter 1** Business context
■ **Chapter 2** Cooperatives, charities and voluntary groups
■ **Chapter 3** Business aims and objectives; Management styles
■ **Chapter 4** The balance sheet
■ **Chapter 5** Industrial relations
■ **Chapter 6** Methods of production
■ **Chapter 7** Product
■ **Chapter 9** The European Union

Questions on Sarah's are asked in:
■ **Chapter 1** Functional areas of business
■ **Chapter 2** Sole traders and partnerships; Franchises
■ **Chapter 4** Breaking even; Financial documents; Profit and loss account

- **Chapter 5** Recruitment; Training, development and appraisal; Motivation
- **Chapter 7** Price
- **Chapter 8** Consumer protection

Information on these businesses is provided below and the appropriate part of the case study is given before the questions.

In addition, a mini case study is provided to offer questions in the style of the **alternative paper to coursework**. This case study, Royaume, is described on pages ix–x. Questions on Royaume are asked in:

- **Chapter 2** Multinationals and holding companies; Public sector businesses
- **Chapter 3** Stakeholders
- **Chapter 4** Cash and cash flow
- **Chapter 5** Rights and responsibilities at work
- **Chapter 6** Management of quality
- **Chapter 8** Measuring customer satisfaction
- **Chapter 9** Fair trade

Questions of the kind likely to be encountered on the **'option' paper** are included as follows:

Business and change questions are on Merrion's Garage Services (pages x–xi) and can be found in:

- **Chapter 2** Limited liability companies
- **Chapter 3** Enterprise and management; Business organisation; Business size and growth
- **Chapter 4** Sources of finance; Costs and revenue; Understanding and using ratios
- **Chapter 5** Pay and benefits
- **Chapter 6** Chain of production
- **Chapter 9** International trade and globalisation

Business communication and marketing questions are on a business called PetsFirst (pages xi–xii) and can be found in:

- **Chapter 1** The operation of markets
- **Chapter 3** Communication; The role of ICT
- **Chapter 6** Business location
- **Chapter 7** Market research; Product life cycles; Promotion; Place (distribution)
- **Chapter 8** Customer service
- **Chapter 9** E-commerce and the internet

Case studies

Fiveways Farm Ltd

Background

Fiveways Farm Ltd is a large dairy farm. It produces milk, cream and cheese, and has recently gone into making bio-yoghurts, which it sells within the European Union. Fiveways has a producer cooperative agreement with five other farms in the county. Dan Farrer owns Fiveways and has just borrowed £50,000 for new machinery to produce the yoghurts. Dan thinks that his venture into yoghurts has been a success and is now thinking of other lines that he might be able to sell. This is called product diversification.

Dan is in charge of all the production. His wife, Janet, is in charge of marketing and sales, while their son, Jeb, is in charge of all the finances and accounts. Jeb can see that the market in 'healthy' foods is growing, and he would like to start up a website to sell the yoghurts online. This would be his own business.

The manager

The farm has recently grown and Dan has employed a manager, Asif, to help him run the business.

Asif has decided that all staff should be trained so that they can be flexible and do each other's jobs when necessary. He has discouraged staff from joining a union. He says that he would rather listen to individual workers than to union representatives. He claims that Fiveways's own policies are actually better and fairer than national policies agreed by unions and management in other parts of the industry.

Asif produces a daily list of tasks for each worker, and a system of records for workers to compile when tasks are complete. The workers, however, are not consulted about the tasks. They are not used to this system and some have objected.

Extract from the balance sheet of Fiveways Farm Ltd (£)

Year	2007	2006	2005
Fixed assets	250,000	240,000	235,000
Current assets	270,000	260,000	245,000
Current liabilities	90,000	85,000	75,000
Net current assets	180,000	175,000	170,000

Sarah's Hairdressing

Planning

Sarah is setting up a hairdressing business. She would like to be able to run the business for herself, as she thinks she knows enough about business to do this. She could set up as an independent business, or could choose to buy a franchise.

Sarah has written a business plan to present to her bank manager in order to raise a loan for the business.

Prices

Sarah has looked at the competitors to her business in the local area and has to make a decision about what sort of prices to charge.

She wanted to know how many standard cut and blow-dries she would have to sell in order to break even. She found that her fixed costs in the first year would be £20,000. The variable cost per cut and blow-dry is £15 and she intends to price them at £25 each.

Staff

Sarah has employed one full-time member of staff to work during the week and three part-time staff to cover weekends. The staff all need an induction training schedule. Sarah also needs to motivate her staff to work well.

Later

Sarah's hairdressing business has now been running for 2 years. She has drawn up the profit and loss account for the previous year's trading, part of which is shown here.

Recently a customer bought a hair dye product from Sarah's shop, but did not ask for any advice about the product. The customer is now demanding her money back, as the colour did not match the outfit she had bought. 'It ruined my evening,' she explained, 'and I think I should be compensated.'

Trading account: Sarah's Hairdressing

		£	£
Sales revenue from hairdressing and product sales			21,000
Minus cost of sales	Opening stock	18,500	
	Plus purchases	5,500	
	Less closing stock	8,000	16,000
Gross profit			**5,000**
Minus expenses	Rent	1,500	
	Wages	2,000	
	Transport	200	
	Power	500	
	Equipment	500	4,700
Net profit			**300**

Royaume Ltd

Background

Royaume Ltd is a worldwide business, specialising in sports equipment, clothing and shoes. Its head office is in Tinnerton, a new town about 25 kilometres from London, but it has operations all around the globe, including other EU countries, North and South America, Asia and the Far East. Royaume operates a 'fair trade' policy. It tries to buy locally sourced materials and makes sure that some of the profits from its operations are ploughed back into the countries where it works.

Organisation

Royaume Ltd is a holding company. It is a private limited company whose shares are owned by the family that founded the business some 25 years ago. Andrew, Pete and Eddy Barrow — three brothers — set up the business and still own 80% of the shares. Many parts of the business have been launched as public limited companies (plcs) when the business needed extra capital or to expand, but the holding company has always kept a controlling interest in each of these. Subsidiaries include Schwitt plc, which specialises in sports shoes.

Schwitt plc

Royaume shoes are produced by Schwitt plc, a subsidiary of the company. The shoes are sold in a very competitive market, among other famous brands such as Nike, Reebok and Adidas. One of Schwitt's main customers is the Royal Navy, which insists on top-quality products. John Young is one of the directors of Schwitt plc and explains, 'We have to walk a very fine line – we want to maintain quality, which means paying for top materials and processes, but we want to keep prices competitive. To maintain our quality, we have introduced a TQM system, rather than the old-style quality checks.'

Cash-flow forecast

Judith Smith works as a financial manager for Schwitt plc and is based in Tinnerton. In June 2007, she prepared the following cash-flow forecast.

	July	Aug	Sept	Oct	Nov	Dec	Cash-flow forecast for Schwitt plc for the last 6 months of 2007 (£000)
Receipts							
Revenue from sales	90	80	75	65	80	160	
Payments							
Wages and salaries	20	20	20	20	20	20	
Materials	20	20	20	20	30	30	
Power and maintenance	10	5	5	10	10	10	
Rent	20	20	20	20	20	20	
Transport	10	10	5	5	5	10	
Advertising	15	10	10	5	10	30	
Total payments	95	85	80	80	95	120	
Net cash flow	−5	−5	−5	−15	−15	40	
Opening balance	25	20	15	10	−5	−20	
Closing balance	20	15	10	−5	−20	20	

Merrion's Garage Services Ltd

Background

Merrion's Garage Services Ltd is a private limited company owned by John Merrion and his family. Merrion's is part of the tertiary sector of the economy. John Merrion says that tertiary sector businesses must 'stay close to their customers'.

Finance

When the company was established, John had three main sources of finance to pay the set-up costs. These were:

- owners' funds
- bank loan
- overdraft

The following is an extract from Merrion's 2007 trading account.

Trading account: Merrion's Garage Services Ltd (£)	2007
Sales revenue	40,000
Cost of sales	22,000
Gross profit	18,000
Profit and loss account	
Gross profit	18,000
Expenses	11,500
Net profit	6,500

Activities

The garage has a scale of charges as shown below.

Standard service	£50.00
Wash and valet	£12.00
Deluxe service (includes wash and valet)	£60.00

Merrion's also buys and sells cars. It recently bought 20 cars from German manufacturers to sell in the UK. The price quoted was £8,000 per car, or €10,000. The exchange rate at the time was €1 = 70p.

The business is currently profitable. Due to its continuing success, Merrion's is thinking of expanding. The business could:

- acquire a rival garage
- diversify into other areas
- merge with a local car showroom

Organisation

Merrion's is organised as shown in the chart below. Three of John's staff form the carwash and valet team. Recently, he has changed the way they are paid from time rate to piece rate.

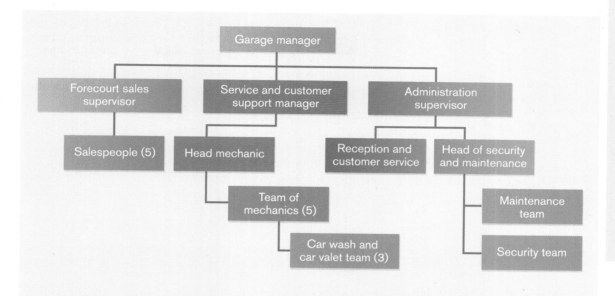

PetsFirst

PetsFirst sells a range of specialist pet foods and pet accessories via a mail order catalogue.

The range of goods sold includes specialist food for dogs, cats and caged birds; toys for dogs and cats; cage toys for budgies; collars; and novelties with pet pictures, such as calendars, tea towels and place mats.

The owners have discussed the following methods of promoting the business:

- 'three for the price of two' offers (the customer buys three products and gets the cheapest one free)
- selling other products, such as cat and dog flaps and bird cages
- providing a 'satisfaction or your money back' guarantee
- providing a monthly newsletter to customers

The owners wanted to find out what other products existing customers might want, so they commissioned a telephone survey comprising 25 key questions. The call centre from which the survey was carried out was based in India and called customers between 7 p.m. and 8 p.m.

PetsFirst currently sells goods only in the UK. The company is considering whether to aim for a wider, international market. This could enable it to sell more and achieve higher profits. However, new technology might be needed to keep up with demand, and distribution costs would rise. The company is also considering setting up a website to sell products over the internet. To do this, it plans to open an e-commerce centre to cope with its web-based sales. This will be over 300 kilometres away from the company's current base, in an Enterprise Zone, where special assistance is available from the government.

The market in which PetsFirst operates is open to competition. A major food company has recently announced that it is to start selling a range of specialist cat and dog food. PetsFirst is considering extending its product range to sell bird cages and is looking at the data shown below (the year is 2010).

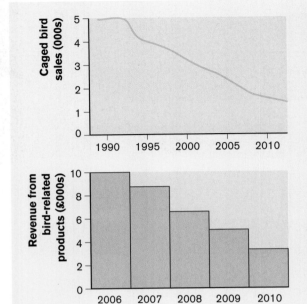

PetsFirst has carried out a SWOT analysis to determine the strength of its market position. The result is shown below.

• Good product range • Quality products • Existing customers • Cater to specialist market	• Specialist market is small • Market is narrow
• Overseas expansion • Internet sales • New markets • New products	• New competition

Chapter 1
Background to business

All businesses operate within a particular context. This means that they have to work with other businesses, and with consumers. They also operate at different levels — local, national and international.

If all businesses 'did their own thing', there would be chaos. There have to be certain rules and expectations within which businesses operate. Context refers to the ways that businesses are expected to behave. It also refers to the ways that businesses and other bodies have to be regulated, by laws, rules and regulations. These include the laws of economics, specifically the way that supply and demand work in markets. The basic organisational shape of most businesses is also an important part of understanding how they work.

Few examination questions ask directly about these contexts and ideas, but they underpin much of what you have studied, so it is useful to include them in answers whenever you can.

Business context

Core knowledge

All businesses have to work within certain sets of rules and behaviours. They are expected to be fair to customers, to staff and to other businesses. They must not make claims for products that they cannot prove; nor can they try to cheat. These conditions are known as the context in which businesses operate. They can usually be split into three areas:
- rules businesses set for themselves
- rules set by government
- rules set by international bodies

Ethics

The rules that businesses set for themselves include what customers expect of them. These rules are often called **ethics** or morals. Acting ethically means doing what appears to be right and fair. Businesses may decide to be friendly to the environment, to treat workers well and to give customers a fair deal. These are all ethical decisions. However, these decisions are likely to benefit a business in other ways, such as increasing its sales or improving its reputation. Businesses may also work

BP's environmental policies are good for its business

within voluntary **codes of conduct** for their own business area — for example, newspaper publishers have rules set by the Press Complaints Commission.

Laws

Government rules are set at both a national and a local level. National rules are usually laid out in laws, or legislation. Local rules are set by bodies such as local authorities and are often called regulations. All these rules are made to protect workers, consumers and other businesses from danger, cheating and unfair treatment. The government has set up bodies such as the **Office of Fair Trading** (OFT) and **Competition Commission** to keep watch where there is a chance of unfair competition. There are also **watchdog** bodies that have been set up to look after consumers' interests.

International laws

As well as local and national rules, there are those set by international organisations. The main international body that affects businesses in the UK is the European Union or EU. The UK is a member of this group of 27 nations and must abide by the decisions it makes. The strength of the EU is such that many other countries want to join it. The UK must also abide by the rules of international trade. Countries gain by trading with each other, but there have to be rules so that stronger countries do not take advantage of weaker ones.

Other external factors

Communities are concerned about factors such as pollution. The benefits of having jobs in the area may be offset by such external costs.

Government policies also affect businesses. The government can help businesses directly through grants, or indirectly through policies designed to increase employment or keep prices stable. Factors like changes in the cost of borrowing money are also

---

Speak the language

code of conduct — a set of rules for a particular business area

Competition Commission — this attempts to ensure that businesses that want to merge, or work together in other ways, are not using their power to be unfair to consumers

ethics — behaving in what is accepted as the right, acceptable or 'moral' manner

Office of Fair Trading — the body set up to investigate unfair trading practices

watchdog — an independent body that looks after consumer interests in certain industries, e.g. Ofwat (the Office for Water) and Ofcom (the Office for Communications)

---

important. The Bank of England sets the level of interest rates each month and any changes affect any business that either has debt or is owed money (i.e. almost every business).

Changes in population size or structure affect businesses too. The UK has an ageing population, meaning a higher proportion of older people. This changes the patterns of demand.

Boost your grade

Few questions will ask directly about the context in which businesses operate, but you can gain higher marks by referring to any of the factors discussed above if they are relevant to the question being asked. For example, in a question on the costs of a business, you could mention changes in interest rates and point out that this is an external factor.

Key points

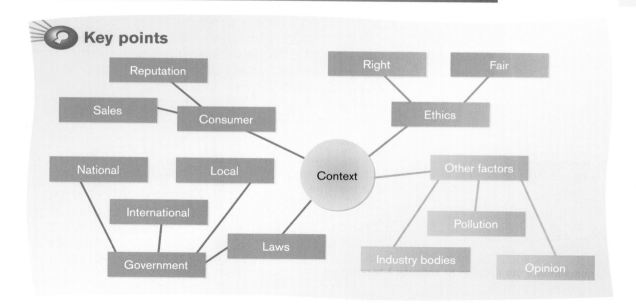

What does the specification require?

Your specification covers the context and functional areas of businesses in both core and option papers, and the material presented in this chapter can appear almost anywhere. The 'External environment' section of the specification covers business activity and competition, ethical considerations and the role of government. The section on 'Aiding and controlling business activity' looks at the reasons for government intervention and the methods by which it might be carried out. Note that detailed knowledge of Acts of Parliament and their dates, EU rules and regulations, and the organisation of government departments, trade unions and pressure groups will not be tested. One area you need to know, however, is the current state of the UK economy: in particular, how it is structured and how this structure is changing (for example, the decline of the primary and secondary sectors and the growth of the tertiary sector).

Regarding material presented in this section, the specification details a number of business contexts. You need to know about business activity in general, and specifically about infrastructure, ethical issues, the environment and how business is regulated and controlled. This includes knowledge of taxation and incentives such as grants and Enterprise Zones, along with external factors such as changes in interest rates. Some legislation, such as that on minimum pay, may be covered, but only in relation to its impact on a particular business, so you must be careful to put answers in the context of the case study.

Test yourself

Read the key terms and their definitions on page 2, then, without looking at them, write a definition of:

➤ business ethics

➤ Office of Fair Trading

➤ Competition Commission

➤ watchdog

Try this

Core paper question

> Fiveways Farm Ltd is a large dairy farm. It produces milk, cream and cheese, and has recently gone into making bio-yoghurts. The demand for these products has grown with advertising claims that they are healthy products and are 'good for you'.
>
> Dan Farrer owns Fiveways and has just borrowed £50,000 for new machinery to produce the yoghurts. Recently, the pressure in the economy has been for interest rates to rise.

Explain how higher interest rates could affect Fiveways. **(4 marks)**

Functional areas of business

Core knowledge

What do businesses do? Essentially, all businesses offer a **product** (a good or service) for sale. Usually they try to sell it at a higher price than that for which they bought it, in order to make a profit. To succeed in this, they need to raise finance so that they can buy or make the product. They then need to let customers know that the product exists and where they can buy it. These actions or functions can be separated into five main areas:

Businesses use local directories to tell customers what they do

- finance
- human resources
- marketing
- production
- administration

All businesses need to carry out these functions, but they are not always in separate departments. A sole trader, for instance, may have to carry out all the functions him or herself.

Finance

This area deals with all aspects of money and accounts. Sometimes it is called 'Accounts'. It arranges and manages the flows of money into, out of and inside a business. It is responsible for raising the funds to start or expand the business and for providing enough money to keep all the other areas operating. This includes setting **budgets**, paying wages and paying bills. The finance function is also in charge of keeping all the financial records of the business. It must make sure they are accurate and available to any official body (such as tax authorities) that needs to see them.

The finance function manages flows of money into and out of a business

Human resources

This area is in charge of everything to do with the people in a business. It hires people, trains them, promotes them if they do well, disciplines them if they break rules and releases them from employment. This can be through termination (the sack),

Speak the language

budgets — financial limits set on processes, products etc.

motivated — happy and wanting to work

product — something that is produced; either a good or a service

reprographic — photocopying and similar jobs

retirement or redundancy. Human resources deals with any official bodies concerned with people in the business, such as trade unions and employment tribunals. It is also responsible for making sure that people are happy, efficient and **motivated**.

Marketing

This area has three main functions linked to customers. It tries to find out what customers want, through market research. Via advertising, it lets customers know that the firm's products are available and where they can buy them. It tries to persuade customers to buy the products of the business by using advertising and promotion.

Production

This area is linked to the manufacture or production of goods. Traditionally, it is in charge of buying raw materials, buying and organising buildings, machines and processes, and ensuring that they all work together efficiently to make the product. Production is also responsible for the quality of parts, processes and the final product. In modern businesses, some of the responsibilities of the production function may be carried out elsewhere — human resources may hire labour, for example. Businesses that sell services, or that act as intermediaries, do not have a production functional area, but still have to maintain efficiency and quality.

Production can only take place with the help of the other functional areas

Administration

This area provides all the service operations that a business needs. These may include: reception; communication (e.g. mail, telephone, face-to-face); filing, **reprographic** and clerical work; organisation and record keeping (e.g. meetings and diaries); cleaning and security. It is also responsible for making sure that the business is operating within company law. In a company, there must be a company secretary who keeps a record of directors' meetings, looks after pensions and insurance, maintains a register of shareholders and keeps the company operating within the law.

Not-for-profit businesses

Some businesses do not try to produce a good or service in order to maximise profit. Instead, they try to maximise returns in other ways. A charity, for instance, may want to maximise the funds it raises; a cooperative may just want to see a fair deal for its members. These businesses still have to carry out the same core functions outlined above.

Boost your grade

Modern businesses are not often divided neatly into these functional areas. For example, much of what used to be administration work is now carried out by managers — they send their own e-mails, for instance, rather than dictating letters. You need to be able to show that you understand that these functions are carried out by all businesses, but are not necessarily divided into areas.

Key points

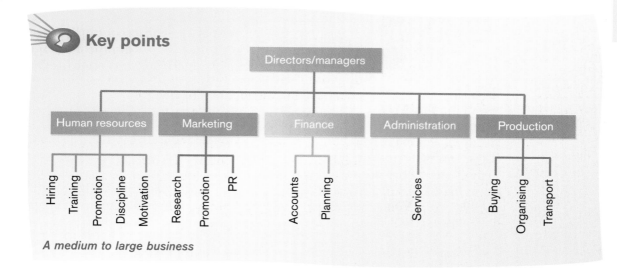

A medium to large business

What does the specification require?

It is unlikely that direct questions on functional areas will be asked. However, you need to know about the relationship of one functional area to another in order to answer questions on organisation and communication. In particular, in the 'Business communication and marketing' option, you need to learn how the marketing department operates in relation to 'new' technology. You need to show awareness of technology such as electronic information and how it is changing businesses, such as through the use of databases and direct mail.

Test yourself

Look at the 'family tree' type diagram of a business above, then close your book and try to recreate it. You may be able to add more jobs or ideas to it.

Try this

Core paper question

> *Sarah is setting up a hairdressing business. She would like to be able to run the business for herself, as she thinks she knows enough about business to be able to do this.*

You are a business adviser whom Sarah has asked for advice. Part of the advice she needs is about the sort of tasks that she might have to carry out, and whether or not she will need help with them. Explain three main tasks that Sarah will have to carry out to run this business. **(6 marks)**

The operation of markets

Core knowledge

All business activity takes place within a framework known as a **market**. A market is anywhere that buying and selling takes place. There are three main types of market:

- *General markets*. All types of product may be bought and sold at these. A car boot sale is a general market, as is a shopping centre.
- *Specialist markets*. These only deal in particular goods or services. Examples are markets for antiques, clothes or fish, and farmers' markets. They also include markets for raw materials and precious metals, such as gold, silver, tin and copper, and services such as shipping and insurance.
  - *Virtual markets*. Not all markets have a physical existence. The website eBay is a good example of how markets can take place in a virtual environment. This is true of many other major markets, including financial markets, insurance markets and share trading.

Just one sort of market – with products, supply and demand

TOPFOTO

All markets, however, work on the same principles. There must be three elements to any market – a product, a supplier of the product, and people or businesses that demand the product.

Demand and supply

The operation of **demand** and **supply** makes markets work. It decides how much of a product is bought and sold, and what price will be paid. The higher the price, the less of a product will usually be demanded. At lower prices, more of a product is demanded. We can therefore show demand as a downward line, sloping from left to right (Figure A, opposite).

A business or supplier is usually willing to supply more at higher prices than at lower prices. Supply therefore slopes upwards from left to right (B).

The two lines cross at the **equilibrium price**. This is the place where both the buyer and the seller agree on the quantity and price, and no forces (of supply or demand) are pushing the price either up or down (C). The buyer is happy to buy that quantity (Q) at that price (P). Similarly, the seller is happy to sell that amount at that price. When markets work efficiently, both buyer and seller are happy.

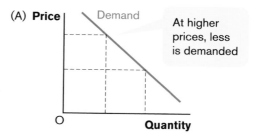

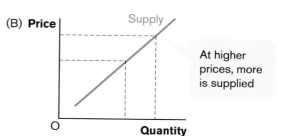

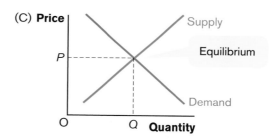

Elasticity

It is important for a business to know the effect a change in price will have on the quantity demanded. Sometimes a small change in price will lead to a big change in demand, in particular where consumers can switch to substitutes. These products are called demand elastic. In other cases, even a large change in price may not affect demand. These products are called demand inelastic. An example is petrol: demand does not respond to a price change because there are few substitutes.

Market structures

Unfortunately, markets do not always work efficiently. Sometimes one business, or a group of businesses, tries to control a market

Speak the language

cartel — where businesses agree to act together to interfere in the normal operation of a market

demand — the amount that consumers want and can pay for

equilibrium price — the point where price settles

market — anywhere that buying and selling takes place

monopoly — where a single business controls a significant part of a market

oligopoly — where a small group of businesses controls a significant part of a market

supply — what a producer is willing to make available in a market

so that it is no longer competitive. The terms **monopoly**, **oligopoly** and **cartel** are used to describe these types of market. If there is little competition and one business gains control of a market, it may be able to restrict supply in order to get higher prices. In the UK, if such markets are against the interests of consumers, government-appointed bodies such as the Competition Commission can stop them. Internationally, such markets are not illegal and their operation can have a great effect on the economies of countries.

Boost your grade

To show your understanding of markets, you need to recognise that sometimes the market system is not appropriate. This may be due to the nature of the product — it might be a necessity, such as water, so it would be unethical and probably illegal to deny it to people because they could not pay for it. If there is a shortage, there might be a system of rationing — during times of drought this happens in the UK. Sometimes countries do not support the market system for strategic reasons — for example, they might want to know that they can produce their own food instead of relying on other countries and trade.

You should also be aware that businesses, through promotion and advertising, are constantly trying to create new markets or manipulate existing ones.

Key points

- The u**P**ward (vertical) axis is **P** for price.
- The level (horizontal) axis is Q for quantity.
- Demand goes *down* from left to right (remember the **D** in **D**emand).
- Supply goes *up* from left to right (remember the **UP** in s**UP**ply).
- Where demand and supply meet, they form an X.
- This is the *equilibrium* point. Think of it as a pair of scales.

- At equilibrium, both consumer and producer are happy.

What does the specification require?

The specification asks that candidates understand the basic economic problem — i.e. how the trade-off between wants and resources results in a price. The option on 'Business and change' includes 'Economic environment', under which heading you need to know about market and mixed economies, different types of competition and why government might need to intervene to control some businesses or industries. In the option on 'Business communication and marketing' you will need, in the section on 'Marketing and the business environment', to draw and interpret graphs showing the changing relationship between demand, supply and price. You should also be able to calculate price elasticity of demand from simple data.

Test yourself

For each case below, say what you think will happen to the price of bread.

➤ When demand for bread falls, ...   *it rises/falls/stays the same*

➤ When the import price of wheat rises, ...   *it rises/falls/stays the same*

➤ When bread is promoted as a healthy product, ...   *it rises/falls/stays the same*

➤ When farmers have a bumper crop of wheat, ...   *it rises/falls/stays the same*

➤ When a new brand of bread is promoted, ...   *it rises/falls/stays the same*

Try this

Question based on the 'Business communication and marketing' option

> PetsFirst sells a range of specialist pet foods and accessories via a mail order catalogue.
>
> A major food company has just announced that it is to start selling a range of specialist cat and dog food.

(a) Label the demand and supply graph below.   **(3 marks)**

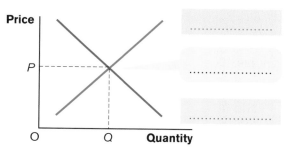

(b) What might happen to the demand for PetsFirst's specialist products. Explain your answer.

(3 marks)

Test on Chapter 1

1 Because consumers demand more as price falls, a demand line:

A slopes down from left to right
B slopes up from left to right
C is horizontal
D is vertical

2 A market that does not have a physical existence, such as sales via the internet, is called:

A virtuous   C general
B virtual   D specialist

3 Because suppliers will supply more as price rises, a supply line:

A slopes down from left to right
B slopes up from left to right
C is horizontal
D is vertical

4 An ethical business stance might not be:

A right   C moral
B acceptable   D profitable

5 Where demand and supply meet, this is called:

A excess demand   C excess supply
B equilibrium   D highest price

6 A market that deals in specific items, like the stock market, is called:

A virtuous   C general
B virtual   D specialist

7 The Office of Fair Trading was set up by:

A the EU   B local councils
C the government D industry

8 The human resources area is not responsible for:

A pensions   B motivation
C budgeting   D training

9 The functional area that deals with transport and obtaining raw materials is called:

A finance   B production
C marketing   D administration

10 Interest rates are set by:

A the EU   C the government
B local councils D the Bank of England

Chapter 2
Owning a business

All businesses are owned by someone or something — usually by people, governments or other businesses. The form of ownership is an important way to distinguish between different businesses.

There are advantages and disadvantages to each type of business structure. Often the type and size of business and the risk that owners are willing to take are important factors in deciding on the type of ownership. Another important factor may be the owner's wish to be independent and make his or her own decisions.

Different types of ownership mean that firms have different numbers of owners, aims, sources of finance, ways of sharing control and profit, and responsibility for debt. When businesses cease to exist they do so in different ways.

Sole traders and partnerships

Core knowledge

Sole traders

A **sole trader** or **sole owner** is a business that is owned and run by one person. The main reason to be a sole trader is often independence. The main aim is usually survival and a modest profit. The owner raises the finance him- or herself from personal sources (**own funds**) or by borrowing. The owner has sole control of the business and makes all the decisions (although, of course, the owner can ask for advice). The owner receives any profit, but is also personally responsible for all the debts of the business.

Examples of sole traders

Advantages versus disadvantages

Sole traders are their own boss. They have independence. They are likely to be better motivated because they are working for themselves. Sole trading is easy and cheap to set up, and no formal paperwork is needed.

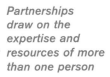

Sole traders carry all the risk and responsibility, so it is difficult for the owner to let other people help with decisions. Raising more money is often hard, so expanding the business may be problematic. Personal possessions are all put at risk should the business fail.

Closing the business

Partnerships draw on the expertise and resources of more than one person

When the owner ceases to trade (through retirement or choice), the business ceases to exist. The owner can also be forced out of business. If he or she is unable to pay the debts of the business, the **creditors** (people owed money) can apply to a court to have the owner declared **bankrupt**.

Partnerships

A **partnership** is a business that is owned jointly by two or more people. Partnerships are often formed so that a business can use more than one person's expertise, or expand to provide a range of services. The owners raise the finance themselves, from personal sources (own funds) or by borrowing. The owners have equal joint control of the business and receive any profit equally unless the Deed of Partnership states otherwise. Responsibility for all the debt of the business is shared among the partners.

Advantages versus disadvantages

A partnership is easy to set up — all it needs is for two or more people to agree to act in partnership. This can be formalised through a written agreement known as the Deed of Partnership. Responsibility is shared, and a partner may bring fresh ideas or different skills.

Partners may fall out and this can harm the business — and the decisions of any one partner are binding on the others. Partnerships have unlimited liability (see below). The business also has no separate legal existence, so if any partner leaves or dies, it ceases to exist.

Closing the business

If any partner leaves, the business ceases to exist and must be re-formed. Partners can also be forced out of the business. If the partners are unable to pay the debts of the business, the creditors can apply to a court to have them declared bankrupt. Each partner is responsible for debt up to the limit of his or her personal wealth.

Liability

Liability is the responsibility of the owner for the debts of the business. It is possible to limit this responsibility, but not all owners do. Sole traders and partnerships have unlimited liability. This means that they are responsible for the debts of the business up to the whole extent that they are able to pay. People and businesses that are owed money by sole traders and partnerships can force the owners to sell possessions in order to pay the debts.

 Key points

	Sole trader	Partnership
Owned by	Single person	Two-plus people
Controlled by	Owner	Partners
Aims	Survival, break even	Break even, expansion
Profits to	Owner	Partners
Liability	Unlimited	Unlimited (usually)
Advantages	Own boss, own decisions, all profit	More expertise, work shared
Disadvantages	Hard work, all risks	Profit shared

Boost your grade

To show your understanding of the detail of small businesses, you should make sure you do not fall into either of the two most common traps:

Sole traders have to work long hours and cannot take holidays.

FALSE. Sole traders can work as and when they wish and can take whatever holidays they like. For some sole traders, this is the very reason why they are in business on their own. If they want the business to continue to operate while they are away, they must employ people to manage it.

Some sole traders are reluctant to do this, as they are still responsible for the business, even if they are not there. Any bad decisions made by managers have to be dealt with by the owner.

Partnerships have to draw up a legal contract.

FALSE. If the Deed of Partnership is not in place, all decision making and profit is automatically shared equally between the partners. A deed is only needed if partners want to vary this automatic equality.

What does the specification require?

Knowledge of the different types of business organisation is central to a good understanding of business studies. However, just having the knowledge is not enough — you must be able to apply it to reach higher mark bands. For instance, it is no use knowing the advantages and disadvantages of sole traders or limited companies if you are unable to say why a particular business might have chosen a particular form of organisation. So, why does that business need to limit its liability? Does it carry a lot of stock, or a lot of risk? Why would it not be appropriate for that business to become a public limited company? Is it too small; does it not really need the capital; is it prepared to lose the possibility of control?

Ownership and control, the subject of Chapter 2 of this book, is covered in the core 'External environment of business' section under the heading 'The organisation', but the greatest emphasis is to be found in section 2 of the specification content, where 'Business structure, organisation and control' is given around 20% of subject content. It is also included in the 'Business and change' option.

Your specification looks at the organisation and ownership of different types of business and concentrates on how and why certain types of organisation or forms of ownership are suitable for particular businesses. With reference to this section, therefore, you should be able to describe the main features and give examples of sole traders and partnerships. The other focus of the specification is on how appropriate the legal and internal structures are when matched to objectives and to future growth. It also looks at how the structure and organisation of businesses is affected by changes in the business environment, such as changes in external factors like the rate of interest or government policy.

Test yourself

List the advantages and disadvantages of forming a partnership.

Try this

Core paper question

> Sarah is setting up a hairdressing business. She will need £25,000 to start it and intends to employ one full-time and two or three part-time staff. She has discussed either setting up on her own, or going into partnership with someone else.

What are the advantages of being a sole trader? What are the advantages of partnership? Would you recommend that Sarah sets up as a sole trader or a partnership? Explain your answer. **(8 marks)**

Limited liability companies

Core knowledge

There are three words in the term **limited liability company** and therefore three things that you need to understand:

- **'Company'** refers to the legal status of the business. It means that the business has been registered with Companies House and is now separated, in law, from its owners.
- **'Limited'** refers to the way in which the responsibility for debt is limited to the amount that a person initially put into the company. If the company can't pay its debts, it is the company that goes bust, not the owners.
- **'Liability'** refers to the responsibility for the debts of the business.

All companies need to be registered with Companies House

Setting up

There must be a minimum of two shareholders to register a business as a company, although there is no maximum. To set up the company, the shareholders draw up a **Memorandum of Association**, giving the name and address of the company and its objectives. This also includes the number of shares issued and therefore what the company is worth. The company must also provide **Articles of Association**, laying down the internal rules of the company. Companies House then provides a **Certificate of Incorporation** and a company registration number.

Advantages versus disadvantages

Businesses become companies to gain limited liability for their owners. This may also help them to raise capital. The separate legal existence of a company means that it can be bought and sold, but this may also be a disadvantage, as it can be taken over.

It is more complicated to set up a company, and rules such as the filing of annual accounts at Companies House must be followed. Accounts and the financial affairs of the company are open to the public. Banks and other financial institutions are less likely to lend to small companies than they are to small businesses with unlimited liability, as the risk of them not getting their money back is higher. Conflicts of interest between groups of shareholders, or between shareholders and management, can also cause problems.

Going public

Companies may be private or public.

- Private limited companies have 'Ltd' after their name, follow rules that are less strict and do not offer shares to the public.
- Public limited companies have 'plc' after their name. They can raise extra money by selling shares to the public. This is called floating a company. In the UK a company seeking to float must offer at least £50,000 worth of shares through an official prospectus detailing the financial situation of the business and future aims.

Aims

The overriding aim of any company is to maximise returns to shareholders. Companies know that if they do not do this, shareholders will lose confidence and sell shares. Share prices will then fall and the company can find itself in trouble.

Speak the language

Articles of Association — the internal rules of the company

Certificate of Incorporation — this sets up the company and establishes liability

company — a business registered at Companies House, with a separate legal existence

limited liability — the owners' responsibility for the debt of the business is limited to the money that they have put into it

Memorandum of Association — legal information on a company, available to the public

---

Boost your grade

Don't forget that whatever a company declares as its objectives (e.g. being environmentally friendly, increasing market share, helping the community, keeping prices down), its main aim will always be to keep shareholders happy. A company that loses shareholders' faith loses value as share prices fall. It may then become a target for takeover, or be unable to continue to trade as customers also lose confidence.

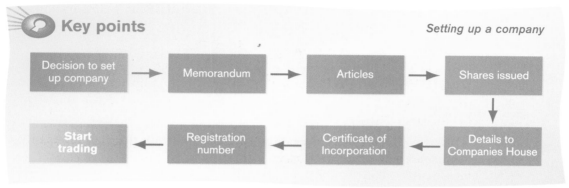

Decision to set up company → Memorandum → Articles → Shares issued

Start trading ← Registration number ← Certificate of Incorporation ← Details to Companies House

What does the specification require?

You should be able to describe the main features and give examples of limited companies, and explain the differences between these and other organisations in terms of objectives, control, sources of finance and distribution of profits. You need to understand what is meant by limited liability and why this might (or might not) be appropriate for particular businesses. This is a particular focus in the 'Business and change' option.

Test yourself

The question paper often opens with some straightforward definitions like the one below. Answers and examples may be drawn from the case study or your own knowledge.

Briefly explain the meaning of the following business term and give an example:

Public limited company   **(5 marks)**

Try this

Question based on the 'Business and change' option

Merrion's Garage Services Ltd is a private limited company owned by John Merrion and his family.

Suggest reasons why this business would want to be a limited company.

(3 marks)

Franchises

Core knowledge

Franchising occurs when a successful business decides to expand by selling the right to other businesses to set up using its ideas. A franchise is a way of starting, owning and operating a business without the high levels of risk associated with other start-ups.

A franchise is a way to organise a business. It is not a form of business ownership. Franchisers are often limited companies or plcs, while franchisees may be sole traders, partnerships or any other form of business ownership.

BSM instructors buy franchises from BSM

The franchise process

There are three key words:

- The **franchise** is permission to sell the product (good or service) or brand, or to use the successful format. There are two parties to the franchise. The franchisee buys the franchise from the franchiser (think 'employer' and 'employee' to get these the right way round).
- The **franchisee** buys into the success of the established business. It buys the use of its name, brand, advertising, reputation and support.
- The **franchiser** is the seller of the franchise. It is the business that has a successful product, brand or format.

Advantages versus disadvantages

Franchisees buy into an established business and may receive help with products, staff, training, marketing and sales materials. They may also gain an exclusive territory, away from competition for the same brand.

Franchisers charge a fee for the franchise and collect a **royalty**, usually based on a percentage of the annual sales of the franchisee. Because a franchisee is buying into a successful product, the fee for the franchise can often be quite high and competition to buy a franchise can be fierce. Franchisers may be quite restrictive, insisting on particular suppliers and making sure that uniforms, products and services are identical.

Why franchise?

Franchises are much safer bets than many other business start-ups. Over 50% of small business start-ups fail in their first year. By contrast, fewer than 1 in 15 franchise outlets stops trading in any one year. Nine out of ten franchises are profitable.

Government

Franchises are also sold by the government or agencies for certain services. Train operators have to buy the franchise to provide particular services; television and radio broadcasters buy the franchise to provide the service in a particular area or over a particular wavelength.

Speak the language

franchise — permission to use a successful business format

franchisee — the buyer of the franchise

franchiser — the seller of the franchise

royalty — a percentage of earnings taken as a fee by the franchiser

🔍 Key points

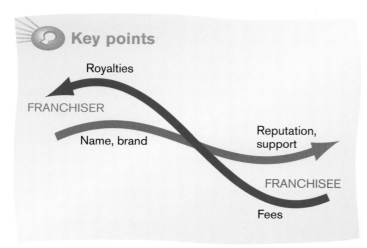

Boost your grade

Think of good examples when writing about franchises. Do not just write about fast-food outlets. In addition, businesses may not necessarily be solely franchise operations. The burger chain McDonald's, for example, owns and operates many of its own outlets — only around a third of its outlets are run as franchises.

What does the specification require?

Franchises are studied under the same headings as other types of business: the likely aims and objectives of the business, funding and liability. They might also be included in questions about how businesses can grow and the advantages and disadvantages that such growth may bring. In the 'Business and change' option, you should study the ways in which internal organisation and communications might be affected by growth.

Test yourself

1 The person who sells a franchise is called the:

   A franchisee   B franchiser   C employer
   D employee   E entrepreneur

2 The person who buys a franchise is called the:

   A franchisee   B franchiser   C employer
   D employee   E entrepreneur

3 The initial payment made to buy a franchise is called a:

A wage   B salary   C fee

D royalty   E cost

4 The ongoing payment that is linked to turnover is called a:

A wage   B salary   C fee

D royalty   E cost

5 Franchises fail in their first year at the approximate rate of:

A 1 in 2   B 1 in 3   C 1 in 4

D 1 in 15   E 1 in 50

Try this

Core paper question

Sarah is setting up a hairdressing business. She could set up as an independent business, but also could choose to buy a franchise.

Explain the advantages and disadvantages of a franchise and recommend whether Sarah should take this option. **(6 marks)**

Multinationals and holding companies

Core knowledge

A multinational is a business that has operations in many countries around the world. It also tends to have a global brand. A typical multinational could be organised like the diagram below.

A **holding company** is one that holds shares in other companies in the same group. The organisational structure of multinationals often includes holding companies. The holding company or **parent company** (e.g. Atlantic Holdings) holds all or most of the shares in each of the **operating companies** (e.g. Windpower plc). Operating companies are also known as **subsidiaries**. Often subsidiaries have their own directors and the rest of their shares might be traded on local stock exchanges, so shares in the US subsidiary in the diagram above might be traded on the New York Stock Exchange.

Why multinationals?

Multinationals benefit from their size. They can buy in bulk. They can also locate operations to keep costs and taxation down. Sometimes production has to be based in certain areas to access markets that would otherwise be protected from them — this has brought several firms within the European Union. Some businesses are almost bound to be multinationals: oil, for example, has to be discovered, extracted, refined and then sold worldwide. Multinationals also benefit from having global brands.

Global brands

A global brand is a brand image that is recognised throughout the world. Brands are of immense value to a business because they help it to be recognised, to gain new markets and to compete against local businesses. The top three brands in 2005 were Coca-Cola, worth around $67 billion (around £36 billion), Microsoft and IBM (all American). The highest-placed non-US brand was Nokia (Finland) at number 6, while the highest UK brand was HSBC at 29 (source: *Interbrand/Business Week*, July 2005).

The world's leading brand in 2005

Criticisms

A multinational may decide to pay tax where its headquarters are based, which could be a country that has low business taxation, rather than where it actually operates. It can also take advantage of low local wage rates and less strict labour laws. Multinationals or **transnationals** have come into conflict with human rights groups, who see them as exploiting labour and natural resources in poorer countries in order to boost profits in richer ones. Multinationals have also been accused of destroying the environment and supporting certain governments and opposing others for their own advantage.

Why holding companies?

Holding companies allow a company to keep control of many different strands of its business. Having companies

Speak the language

holding company — a company that holds all or most of the shares in other companies

operating company — a company that produces and trades

parent company — another name for the top company in a group

subsidiaries — businesses that are owned by holding companies

transnational — another word for a multinational

in separate business units helps the holding company to see which are profitable and to direct expertise where it is needed. Holding companies act like puppeteers. They hold the strings and can cut them to get rid of poor performers or buy in new companies to strengthen weaker areas. Often holding companies do not produce anything, but exist purely to hold shares in other businesses.

Boost your grade

You can show your depth of knowledge by including details such as the fact that some holding companies are plcs and quoted on stock exchanges, whereas others may be a way for a family company to keep control. In the second case, the holding company may be a private limited company. For example, Virgin Group Limited — the parent company of Virgin — is a private limited company although many Virgin subsidiaries are plcs.

Key points

- Holding companies enable a business to keep control of a number of other businesses.
- Multinationals are often organised in this way.
- Multinationals operate in a number of countries.
- Sometimes multinationals are richer and more powerful than the countries in which they operate, and this can cause problems.
- Multinationals are often criticised for avoiding tax, taking advantage of cheap labour and destroying the environment, but they would defend themselves against these charges.

What does the specification require?

In the section on 'Business structure, organisation and control', the specification asks you to describe the main features and give examples of holding companies, to identify the reasons for the importance and growth of multinational businesses and to explain, in terms of objectives, control, sources of finance and distribution of profits, the differences between these and other business organisations.

Test yourself

Read the key terms and their definitions on page 23, then, without looking at them, write a definition of:

➤ holding company
➤ operating company
➤ subsidiaries

➤ parent company
➤ transnational

Try this

Alternative paper to coursework question

> *Royaume Ltd is a worldwide business, specialising in sports equipment, clothing and shoes. Royaume Ltd is a holding company. Many parts of the business have been launched as public limited companies (plcs) when the business needed extra capital, or to expand, but the holding company has always kept a controlling interest in each of these.*

Explain why Royaume Ltd has expanded through holding companies while itself staying in private ownership. **(8 marks)**

Public sector businesses

Core knowledge

A **public sector** business is one that is government-owned. It is called 'public' because the government owns or operates it on behalf of the public. The public sector used to be a very important part of the UK economy, but over the years it has become much smaller as many public sector businesses have been sold into private ownership. This process is called **privatisation**.

Why public?

There are a number of reasons for governments — at a local, regional or national level — to own or operate businesses. These include the following:

- *National security.* Some services could be dangerous if in private hands. These include defence and the armed forces.
- *Politics.* Sometimes there are political reasons for keeping a particular business out of private hands. This could be to prevent foreign takeovers of vital industries, for example.
- *Social.* The government might choose to own a business so that it can subsidise the business and make sure that employment or services are provided where it would not be economic for a private business to do so.

A debate in the House of Commons

Speak the language

privatisation — taking previously public businesses and industries and selling them into private hands

public sector — businesses and industries owned/operated by government

watchdog — an independent body that makes sure an industry is acting fairly, e.g. Ofwat (the Office for Water)

- *Charging.* Sometimes it is virtually impossible to charge fairly for services, so they must be paid for out of local or national taxation. For example, how could each individual 'user' be charged for his or her use of street lighting?
- *Economics.* Some services need to be provided where it is not possible for a private business to make a profit.
- *Monopolies.* If a business has a monopoly — and the service is essential — governments may step in to make sure that customers are not exploited.

In many cases, where companies remain privately owned, **watchdog** bodies have been appointed to make sure that they operate fairly.

Privatisation

Governments from 1980 onwards decided that, providing there were sufficient safeguards, many public sector industries could be sold into private hands. They believed that this would save tax money and that the businesses would run more efficiently in private hands. In many cases, competition was created by breaking up the public sector industry. As a result there are now, for example:

- a number of telecommunications providers instead of just the Post Office and BT
- a number of different power suppliers instead of just British Gas and the regional electricity boards
- several different train companies 'competing' on centrally owned track, instead of British Rail

Who pays for public industry?

How could a business make a profit from collecting rubbish?

The public sector is funded from taxation in three main ways:

- General taxation, such as income tax, is used to pay for central government services.

- Local taxation, such as business rates and council tax, is used to pay for local services.
- National Insurance contributions are used to pay for the health service, pensions and other benefits.

Services

The public sector is the main employer in the key services: health, education and social services.

- *The health service.* Although private suppliers and competition between health authorities are encouraged, the health service is still free for people when they need it, paid for by National Insurance contributions.
- *The civil service.* These are people employed directly by the government to administer government policy at local and national level.
- *Social services.* These are individual and family support services which, again, are free at the point of need.
- *Education.* Although there are private fee-charging schools to which people may choose to send their children, education up to 18 is still provided free for everyone, paid for out of taxation.

Boost your grade

Privatisation of public sector industries is no longer a hot topic, so it is unlikely to be examined. However, partial privatisation is still controversial. This happens when private finance is brought in to support public spending. PFI (the Private Finance Initiative) and PPP (Public–Private Partnerships) are ways to introduce private money and competition into areas like the health service and road building. For example, a private contractor built the UK's first motorway toll road (where drivers pay to use the road) and collects the tolls. Do you think that this is a good thing?

Key points

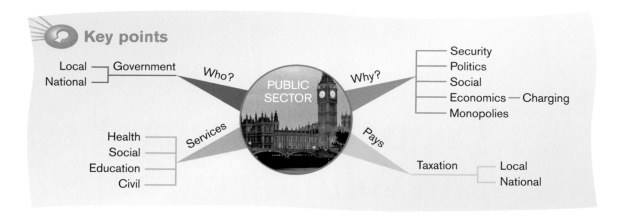

What does the specification require?

Although public sector businesses used to form a major part of the UK economy, there are now few left, so this area no longer carries the importance that it used to. Your specification looks at the public sector in the section on the 'External environment of business' and asks you to be able to explain the differing aims of private and public sector organisations in the UK, even though these may be historical. You should also be aware of changes that have taken place in the relative size and structure of the UK public sector in the last few years and know of any recent changes in private and public ownership. You should understand the role of government in business activity and the agencies through which it carries out this role.

Test yourself

Look at the two lists below. Match each reason for public ownership with the correct example.

Reason	**Example**
1 national security	**a** it is not possible to put a fair price on the service
2 social	**b** nuclear weapons
3 politics	**c** preventing a business from exploiting customers
4 charging	**d** providing employment where it is needed
5 monopolies	**e** preventing foreign takeovers

Try this

Alternative paper to coursework question

Royaume shoes are produced by Schwitt plc, a subsidiary of the company. One of Schwitt's main customers is the Royal Navy, which insists on top-quality products.

The Royal Navy is in the public sector. Explain what this classification means.

(3 marks)

Cooperatives, charities and voluntary groups

Core knowledge

Most businesses try to make a profit. In some special cases, however, businesses do not want to make a profit.
- **Cooperatives** and **mutual societies** want to make sure that their members all get a fair deal.
- **Charities** want to maximise the amount of good that they can do. This usually means raising as much money as possible for their particular cause.

- Voluntary groups usually provide a service to the community. People volunteer to work for them, for no pay. Examples include St John's Ambulance and the Royal National Lifeboat Institution. These groups may also be supported by charitable donations.

VG retailing

Another sort of voluntary group involves a number of retailers or similar small businesses joining together voluntarily to gain some of the benefits of big business. Several shops, for example, can gain the benefit of lower prices from large orders, which would not be available to each individual shop. In the UK these groups include Nisa, VG and SPAR.

Cooperatives

Each member of a cooperative puts in the same amount of money to set up the business. Each shares equally in the control of the business and takes an equal share of the profits. In larger cooperatives, management control may fall to a smaller group, but these people will be elected by all the membership. The main types of cooperative are as follows:

One machine can be shared by several farmers

- *Worker cooperative.* A group of workers pool their labour to produce a good or service.
- *Producer cooperative.* A group of producers share costs and help each other to sell produce. These are often agricultural and share expensive machinery which each needs only for a short time. They can also get better prices for products if they all offer similar prices.
- *Consumer cooperative.* These are generally retail organisations that buy goods and services on behalf of members and make sure that they are sold at fair prices.

Mutual societies

These were set up to provide members with financial help. Originally they were insurance societies (protecting against fire or theft), building societies (to help members buy houses) and even funeral societies (to pay for funerals and provide pensions). Many have now grown into big businesses and become household names — for example, Scottish Widows or Halifax Bank plc.

Speak the language

charity — a 'business' that tries to do the most good for its chosen cause

cooperative — a group that shares in a business to ensure a fair deal for its members

mutual society — a society set up to provide benefit to its members

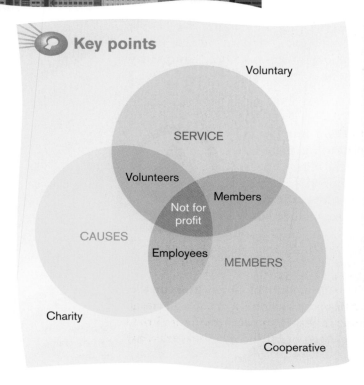

Key points

Voluntary

SERVICE

Volunteers

Members

Not for profit

CAUSES

Employees

MEMBERS

Charity

Cooperative

What does the specification require?

Not-for-profit businesses are studied under the same headings as other types of business: the likely aims and objectives of the business, funding and liability. Questions may focus on the ethical and moral reasons for organisations such as cooperatives, mutuals and charities, and on how they raise finance, are organised and distribute profits.

Test yourself

1 Which of the following do members of a cooperative share equally: (a) profits; (b) decision making and control; (c) risk?

A (a) and (b) only   B (a) and (c) only   C (b) and (c) only
D all of these   E none of these

2 Which of the following is not a type of cooperative?

A worker   B consumer   C producer
D mutual   E charity

3 Nisa, VG and SPAR in the UK are examples of:

A volunteer groups   B voluntary groups   C supermarket chains
D discount clubs   E charities

4 A mutual society is set up to provide benefits to its:

   A shareholders   B customers   C suppliers
   D members   E workers

5 Charities are set up to maximise:

   A profits for a cause   B revenue for a cause   C good for a cause
   D market share for   E publicity for
     a cause   themselves

Try this

Core paper question

Fiveways Farm Ltd is a large dairy farm. It produces milk, cream and cheese,
and has recently gone into making bio-yoghurts. Fiveways has a producer
cooperative agreement with five other farms in the county.

(a) What is meant by 'producer cooperative'?   **(2 marks)**
(b) Explain how such a cooperative would work and how the farms could
     benefit from it.   **(4 marks)**

Test on Chapter 2

Copy and complete the sentences below.

1 A .... is a business that is owned and run by one person.

2 A partnership is a business that is owned by .... people jointly.

3 In a partnership, the owners have equal joint control of the business unless the ....
   states otherwise.

4 .... means the responsibility of the owner for the debts of the busines

5 There must be a minimum of .... shareholders to register a business as a company.

6 To set up a company, shareholders must draw up a ...., giving the name and
   address of the company and its objectives.

7 Companies House then provides a .... and a company registration number.

8 A .... business is one that is government-owned.

9 The person selling a franchise is called the ....

10 Public limited companies can raise extra money by selling shares to the public. This is called .... a company.

11 Franchising is when a successful business decides to .... by selling the right to other businesses to set up using its ideas.

12 Franchisers charge a fee for the franchise and collect a ...., usually based on a percentage of the annual sales of the franchisee.

13 A society set up to provide benefit to its members is called a ....

14 A .... is one that holds shares in other companies in the same group.

15 A .... is a business that has operations in many countries around the world.

16 When public sector businesses have been taken into private ownership, a .... body is usually set up to protect consumers.

17 The public sector is funded from ....

18 .... want to maximise the amount of good that they can do, which usually means raising as much money as possible for their particular cause.

19 When a group of workers pool their labour to produce a good or service, this is called a ....

20 The person buying a franchise is called the ....

Chapter 3
Managing a business

This chapter covers setting up, organising and managing a business. Businesses operate in different ways according to the type of product they produce, the service or sector that they are in, their size and the way in which their owners or managers feel comfortable working.

Enterprise has become increasingly important. The government wants a dynamic economy and realises that there are not always enough jobs to go around. The promotion of an enterprise culture helps with both these issues. In an enterprise culture there are many people trying new things and introducing new goods and services. There are also many people who are working for themselves rather than for an employer, and who are, in effect, creating their own jobs. Because of its importance, enterprise is featuring more often on examination papers, so understanding how to set up and run a business is very important.

Enterprise and management

Core knowledge

Businesses would not exist unless people were willing to take risks. People who set up new businesses are usually known as **entrepreneurs** and the quality that they are showing is called **enterprise**. Entrepreneurs are those who can think of a business idea and have enough confidence to try to make it work. This could involve risking their own money, or persuading other

Three well-known entrepreneurs: Richard Branson (Virgin), Anita Roddick (The Body Shop) Stelios Haji-Ioannou (easyJet)

people, such as banks, to lend them money. They set up, organise and manage the business, and hope that it will be profitable. Entrepreneurs are often called the fourth factor of production as it is they who organise land, labour and capital — the factors of production — to make the business a success.

Why bother?

Not everyone is cut out to be an entrepreneur. Many people are happy to work for others and never take business risks. So what makes some people want to start a business? Reasons include:

- independence — the desire to work for themselves
- the pleasure that comes with success
- a higher income, as long as the business makes a profit
- using their skills, knowledge or experience
- needing new challenges to keep them on the ball

Business failure

However hard entrepreneurs try, some of them will fail. Usually this is because the business idea was not very good, someone else got to the market first (competition) or the business was poorly planned. The main reasons for failure are:

- not including all costs
- taking on too much debt
- not meeting customers' needs
- not having the right skills, knowledge or experience
- being over-optimistic about sales
- being unable to pay suppliers or other business debts

Why is management needed?

People do not automatically do what they are supposed to do, or carry out jobs in the most efficient or effective manner.

Speak the language

delegation — passing authority or responsibility on to other people, so that they can carry out a function on your behalf

enterprise — the ability to succeed in business, through taking risks

entrepreneur — a person who is willing to take risks to bring about business success

management — the process of making sure that people are doing the right jobs at the right time in the right way

Businesses therefore need to be organised and managed. Even a sole trader has other people whom he or she has to deal with, who may need managing. These could include suppliers, employees, agents — in fact, any group working on the sole trader's behalf that has a link to the business.

Time management

One of the most important areas of **management** for anyone in business is the ability to be able to manage their own time. For sole traders this can be the crucial difference between success and failure. Time management means having the self-discipline to know when jobs need to be done by, and to make sure that enough time is devoted to them.

Delegation and trust

In big businesses there are whole groups of people who need managing. Even in small businesses the owner may need to **delegate** responsibility to other people and trust them to get on with the job. Many students wrongly state that sole traders are unable to take holidays or breaks. This is not true. However, for the business to continue to operate, the trader needs to employ someone whom he or she knows is trustworthy and capable of doing the job. In bigger businesses this delegation of responsibility is a formal part of some people's jobs.

Boost your grade

The link between organisation, management and stakeholders is an obvious one, but you could gain more marks by being able to describe the link — the fact that stakeholders and the business rely on each other — in detail.

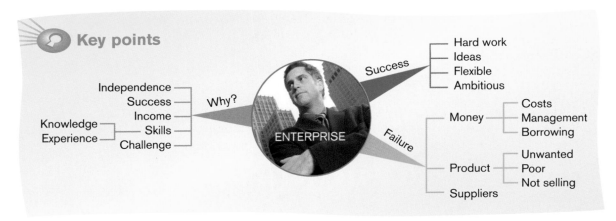

Key points

What does the specification require?

The idea of enterprise and management is a major theme. Organisational areas are included in the section on 'Business structure, organisation and control', and it is here that you will need to know about organisation charts, internal communication, hierarchies, and roles and responsibilities in a business. The 'Business and change' option looks at business size and growth, and at how changes in ownership or size can have management implications. The 'Business communication and marketing' option covers key elements of internal and external communication.

Enterprise is a key area of all business studies specifications. It is important to know and understand the role of the entrepreneur in creating wealth and providing employment, and the role of the manager in motivating and encouraging success. You should be aware of the criteria against which businesses (and entrepreneurs) judge their success, such as survival, expansion, the creation of wealth, profitability and job creation. You also need to understand about the qualities of an entrepreneur, what is meant by risk-taking and the reasons for the success or failure of a business.

Test yourself

Read the key terms and their definitions on page 34, then, without looking at them, write a definition of:

➤ enterprise ➤ entrepreneur

➤ management ➤ delegation

Try this

Question based on the 'Business and change' option

> Merrion's Garage Services Ltd is a private limited company owned by John Merrion and his family. The business is currently profitable.

Explain what the owners of the business might do with the profit. **(5 marks)**

Stakeholders

Core knowledge

Businesses can only exist if people take risks. The owners of a business are usually the ones who take the risk. But once a business does exist, there are many people, other than the owners, who have an interest in its success (or failure). Stakeholders are people who have a stake in a business.

Internal stakeholders

Some stakeholders have a direct interest in the business. These are the people who are employed by it or who own it. They rely on the business for their income and are called **internal stakeholders**.

Owners

Owners may be a single person (sole trader), a group of people (partnerships, cooperatives), another business (institutional owners, holding companies), government (public sector businesses) or shareholders. Owners want success and profit.

Many groups are affected by the operation of a business

Shareholders are a special group of owners. Each has a share of the business. In a small business, they may also be the managers. In private limited companies, shareholders are usually restricted to family and friends, but a public limited company may have thousands of shareholders. Many of these shareholders have little or nothing to do with the business — they just take their share of the profits (called a **dividend**) if it is successful. If a company is not successful, shareholders can sell their shares and buy those of another business.

Employees

Employees want a fair day's pay for a fair day's work in decent conditions. They may also want some say in how the business is run. They have the right to fair and equal pay and treatment, and should also be given opportunities for training and promotion.

Managers are the link between the employers and the employees. In some ways, they share the wants of both. Managers want success for the business, as this reflects well on their own management skills. They also want good, reliable employees to make sure the business keeps being successful.

External stakeholders

External stakeholders are people or other businesses that have a less direct stake in a business. For example, the business might be located in their community, they might buy its products, they might compete with it or they might supply the business. The main groups of external stakeholders are as follows:

Speak the language

dividend — a share of a business's profits, divided according to the number of shares owned

external stakeholders — people or other businesses that have a less direct stake in a business than internal stakeholders

internal stakeholders — those with a direct interest in a business, e.g. owners, employees

managers — employees in a position of responsibility who provide the link between ordinary employees and owners

quality — this refers to products that are fit for purpose: they do what they should do (it does not mean 'expensive')

shareholders — those who own shares in a business

- *Customers*. Without these the business could not exist; they want **quality** and reliability.
- *Suppliers*. These need to supply quality products and parts. They want to work with businesses that order regularly and pay promptly.
- *Financial stakeholders*. These are people or institutions (e.g. banks) that have lent the business money. Suppliers may also fall into this group if they supply goods on credit. They want a sound business that is able to pay them back.
- *Community*. The area where the business operates may suffer from business problems such as transport and pollution, but can benefit from the provision of employment. The community wants the benefits to outweigh the problems.
- *Government*. Local and national governments regulate and control businesses, making sure that they operate within the law. They also collect tax to provide services for both businesses and the community.
- *Pressure groups*. These work to bring about particular changes, such as more sustainable farming, less pollution, safer and better working conditions and other benefits.

Key points

Owners

Shareholders

Managers

INTERNAL

Employees

Pressure groups

STAKEHOLDERS

Customers

Banks

EXTERNAL

Creditors

Community

Suppliers

Government

Conflicts

Sometimes stakeholder groups have conflicting aims. For example, customers may want lower prices while shareholders want higher profits; suppliers may want paying immediately while the business wants to delay payment; a business may want to expand operations while the community would like to keep it small. Balancing these aims so that all groups are happy is one of the skills of a manager.

Boost your grade

Make sure that you do not confuse stakeholders with shareholders. All shareholders are stakeholders in the businesses in which they have bought shares, but few stakeholders are shareholders.

What does the specification require?

Under the section on the 'External environment of business', the specification asks you to be able to explain the roles of the different stakeholder groups involved in business, and especially cites owners, producers, consumers, employees, government and taxpayers.

Test yourself

Draw a spider diagram with the name of a local business in the centre and write the names of its major stakeholders around it. Show which are internal and which are external stakeholders.

Try this

Alternative paper to coursework question

> Royaume Ltd is a worldwide business, specialising in sports equipment, clothing and shoes. Its head office is in Tinnerton, a new town about 25 kilometres from London, but it has operations all around the globe, including other EU countries, North and South America, Asia and the Far East.

Name two stakeholders or stakeholder groups that would be interested in the activities of Royaume. Explain why they would be interested in the business. **(8 marks)**

Business aims and objectives

Core knowledge

Businesses need to know whether or not they are making progress or succeeding in what they are trying to do. To find this out, they have to measure their progress. Progress can be measured by using aims and objectives. Sometimes this is easy — a football club can measure its progress by how high up the league it gets. But this is not the only thing it will need to measure — it also needs to know how financially successful it is, whether it can pay its wages, how it can attract more fans, and so on.

A football club can measure its progress by its position in the league

Aims

Businesses usually set themselves a long-term goal, called an aim, which they would like to reach. This is often something they will only ever be able to work towards. Sometimes the aim of a business is contained in its **mission statement** or **vision**. Aims are often general: 'being the best in the world', 'being a friend to the environment', 'creating new and exciting products' are all examples.

Objectives

The steps on the way to achieving an aim are marked by shorter-term objectives or targets. Objectives are usually more clearly defined than aims. Often the steps on the way to reaching an objective are called targets.

SMART targets

SMART helps people remember what characteristics targets should have in order to be useful. Targets should be:
- **S**pecific — they should be definite
- **M**easurable
- **A**chievable — there is no point having targets that can never be reached
- **R**ealistic and relevant
- **T**ime related — targets should be achieved within a set time period

Maximum aims versus minimum aims

Some aims involve making the *most* of something. These are called **maximising aims**. The central aim of most businesses is to maximise profit. Other areas that a business might seek to maximise are:
- sales revenue
- market share
- growth

Other aims may involve making the *least* of something. These are called **minimising aims**. A business might aim for:
- low employee turnover
- low numbers of complaints
- the least possible impact on the environment

Small businesses

Small businesses often have less far-reaching aims than large businesses. It is likely that they will want to:

Key points

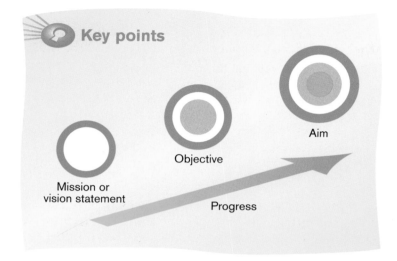

Aim

Objective

Mission or
vision statement

Progress

- survive as a business
- reach a breakeven point at which costs are covered

Owners may also want to achieve other aims, such as independence, a good reputation and loyal customers. Some of these are called **satisficing aims**. A small business may, for example, want to make enough income to stay in business, and be satisfied with this. Not all the owners of small businesses want them to grow into bigger ones.

What does the specification require?

You need to be able to identify suitable aims for a business and to say how targets and objectives can be used to reach these aims. Aims include survival, growth, profitability, wealth creation and market share, and their relationship with each other and with the size of the business. In the 'Business and change' option, you should be able to describe how aims for each form of business organisation might develop and change. This also concerns the effects of ratio-nalisation on both the business and its customers.

Test yourself

1 Long-term goals of businesses are usually called:

A aims   B objectives   C targets
D smart targets   E progress points

2 Short-term goals of businesses are usually called:

A aims   B objectives   C targets
D smart targets   E progress points

3 A mission statement is used by a business to:

A help customers choose products
B help show the aims of the business
C help shareholders see how well the business is doing
D help suppliers see what the business wants
E fool competitors

4 The 'A' in 'SMART target' stands for:

A allowable   B acceptable   C adequate
D achievable   E ample

5 The 'T' in 'SMART target' stands for:

A time related   B timed target   C target
D technical   E token

Try this

Core paper question

> Fiveways Farm Ltd is a large dairy farm. It produces milk, cream and cheese, and has recently gone into making bio-yoghurts. Dan Farrer owns Fiveways and his son, Jeb, works for him. Jeb can see that the market in 'healthy' foods is growing, and he would like to start up a website to sell the yoghurts online. This would be his own business.

Explain the objectives that Jeb might set for his first year.   **(6 marks)**

Business organisation

Core knowledge

For any business to operate, it needs to have some sort of structure. Businesses can be organised in a number of different ways. How they are organised usually depends on their size, the management style of the owners, the type of business or the type of market they are in.

Functions

All businesses have to carry out a number of **functions** in order to operate. These include finance, marketing and sales, administration, production, customer service and human resources, along with communication between the various functions. One of the main forces that affects organisation structure is the way that a business decides to carry out these functions.

Small businesses

In a small business it is unlikely that the functions will be divided into separate areas. If the business is a sole trader, the owner will carry out many of the functions personally, but there is nothing to prevent him or her bringing in an expert to help. For example, a consultant might advise on marketing and sales, an accountant might look after financial aspects and an agency might be used to hire staff. Decisions are likely to be taken centrally, by the owner in a sole trader, the partners in a partnership, the members of a cooperative or the small group of shareholder-directors in a private limited company.

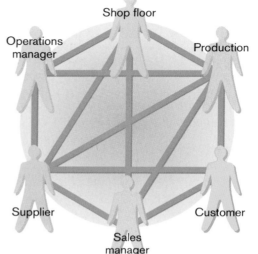

A particular project may need skills and expertise from many different areas

Larger businesses

Larger businesses need a more formal organisation structure. This is likely to be based on the functional areas of a business, but may also be arranged according to one of the following:

- geography — where the various parts of the business are located
- product — what each part of the business makes
- process — what each part of the business does in the chain of production

Organisation charts

Charts can show how a business is organised. The most common type is the 'family tree' chart, showing each 'family' of workers under a manager or director. Each manager has a number of people under his or her control.

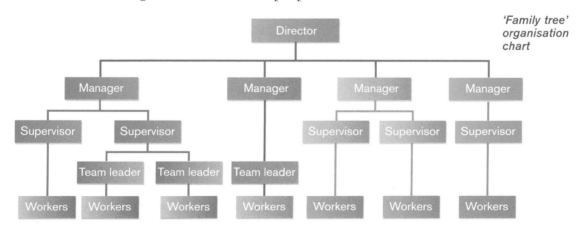

'Family tree' organisation chart

Span of control of manager

'Span of control' organisation chart

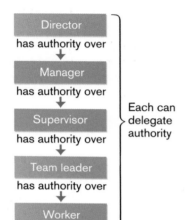

Authority and delegation

Vertical versus horizontal organisational structure

This is called the **span of control** and may be wide or narrow. The narrower the span, the greater the power the manager has over those underneath — his or her subordinates.

The power of a manager in a business is usually called **authority** — the right within the organisational set-up to make decisions. In some cases, this authority may be passed on. This is called **delegation**. In an organisation that is very centrally controlled, there is little delegation, and all decisions are made at the top.

Vertical organisations

Most organisations are hierarchical. This means that the people at the top have more authority than those at the bottom. There are also usually fewer people at the top than at the bottom. This type of organisational structure is called a **hierarchical pyramid**. Some businesses have a very vertical structure. This means that there are many layers but few people at each layer. Communication up and down a vertical structure may be slow if it has to pass through all the layers.

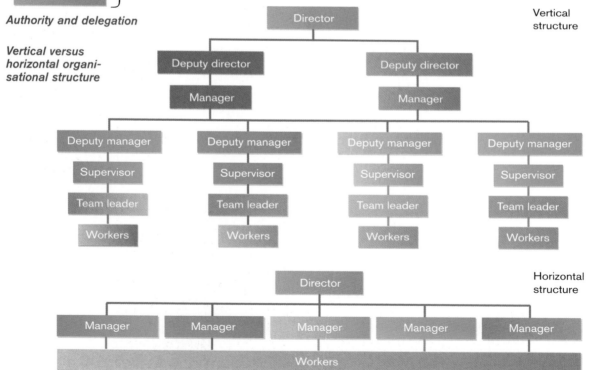

Managing a business

Horizontal organisations

Some businesses have a horizontal structure. This means that there are few layers and many people in each layer. Although communication within each layer is therefore generally good, this sort of structure can make decision making hard. Many cooperatives, for example, have a single layer, and all members have an equal say. All major decisions need to be agreed by all the members, which can be inefficient.

For some projects it is important to use a variety of skills drawn from many parts of the business. This type of organisational structure is called a matrix structure.

Speak the language

authority — the power to make decisions

delegation — passing authority to others

functions — the types of task that have to be carried out in a business

hierarchical pyramid — a structure consisting of layers of power, with fewer people and more power at the top

span of control — the number of people for whom a manager is directly responsible

Key points

- All businesses need to be organised.
- All businesses, of whatever size, have to carry out the business functions.
- The bigger the business, the more likely it is to need a formal organisational structure.
- The type of organisational structure can both help and hinder efficiency.

Boost your grade

Businesses have both formal and informal organisational structures. The formal structure is that which is laid down by the management. It says who has what power and authority, and over whom, and how actions should be carried out. The informal structure — groups of friends who socialise or play sport together, for example — may be more powerful than the formal structure. Mentioning this possibility in an answer about organisation will earn higher marks.

What does the specification require?

Internal organisation structures are studied under the heading of 'Business structure, organisation and control'. You should be able to draw simple organisation charts and explain how they work. This includes the roles, responsibilities and interrelationships of people within organisations, and the use of specialist terms such as span of control, departments, delegation and communication. The 'Business and change' option asks you to be able to describe the structure of business organisations in terms of their ownership and financial structure and the ways in which these may change — for example, through growth or as a result of external factors.

Test yourself

Read the key terms and their definitions on page 45, then, without looking at them, write a definition of:

➤ functions   ➤ span of control   ➤ hierarchical pyramid

➤ authority   ➤ delegation

Once you have completed and checked your definitions, write a sentence that puts each key term into context.

Try this

Question based on the 'Business and change' option

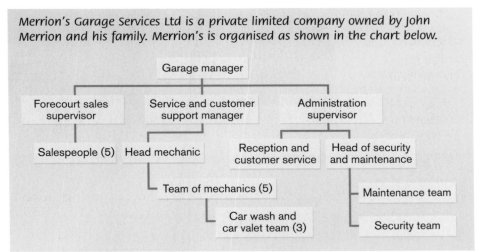

Merrion's Garage Services Ltd is a private limited company owned by John Merrion and his family. Merrion's is organised as shown in the chart below.

(a) How many layers are there in the chain of command between the garage manager and the car wash team? **(1 mark)**

(b) Explain the term 'span of control'. Give an example from the chart. **(3 marks)**

Business size and growth

Core knowledge

Businesses can be very small — sole traders with no employees — or very large, employing thousands of people. To get from one to the other requires growth. Businesses can grow internally by increasing market share or product range, for example, or externally by joining with other businesses. But how do you know if one business is bigger than another?

Measuring size

The size of a business can be measured in different ways, but each way has to be treated with care.

Measurement	Caution
Number of employees	A big business may use a lot of machines and not need many workers.
Value of assets	Adding up the value of everything a business owns does not show you its real size — this is only possible by comparing it with rival businesses. Some assets may be hard to value — a trade name or reputation, for example.
Value on stock market (value of each share × no. of shares issued)	This kind of valuation is only possible for a public limited company. Even then, shares may be traded for many reasons, affecting the price. If the share price changes, does this mean that the size of the business has changed?
Size of **sales revenue**	A business that sells one diamond a year may have higher sales revenue than one that sells 10,000 smaller stones — but which is bigger?
Share of market	A business with a small share of a large market may be bigger than one with a large share of a small market.

Small or large?

Because of the problems of defining business size, businesses are usually defined as small, medium or large according to the measures shown in the table below.

	Employees	Revenue	Assets
Small	Fewer than 50	Less than £2 million	Less than £1 million
Medium	50–249	£2–8 million	£1–3 million
Large	250+	£8 million+	£3 million+

SMEs

SMEs stands for small and medium-sized enterprises. This is a special group of businesses that the government tries to help. Their size is defined by their number of employees (up to 249), a definition that includes micro businesses with fewer than 10 employees.

Growth

A business can get bigger through either **internal growth** or **external growth**.

- Internal growth occurs when a business grows larger from within by increasing sales, using new technology, widening its product range or expanding its markets.
- External growth occurs when a business grows by joining with other businesses. It can either merge with other businesses (**merger**) or take over another business (**takeover**).

Key points

- It is difficult to say, with certainty, whether a business is big or small.
- It helps to look at the type and size of market the business is in.
- Governments use fairly standard measures to help define size.
- Not all businesses want to grow bigger.
- If they do, they can grow internally or externally.

Why stay small?

Many businesses do not try to grow. If they have just started they might be more concerned with survival. There are around 4 million small businesses in the UK. A business might stay small if:

- it is already achieving its objectives without getting any bigger
- it is providing a local service — window cleaning or hairdressing, for example
- it is supplying specialist products to small markets

Boost your grade

You might have the chance to introduce the idea of *integration* into an answer. This is the technical term for a business joining with another. The types of integration are shown here. The important thing to remember is what advantages integration might bring — for example, bigger market share, economies of scale, greater specialisation, removing competition and securing supplies.

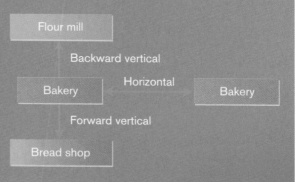

What does the specification require?

Business size and growth are covered in several parts of the specification. For example, in 'External environment of business', the section on 'The changing business environment' looks at different ways of measuring the size of businesses. You should be able to select and justify an appropriate way to measure the size of a particular business.

You should also be aware of the problems of growth — in terms of the organisation, its management, stakeholders and communications. The 'Business and change' option looks at the internal organisation of a business and the ways in which it might change with growth, and asks you to be able to explain the effects of changes in areas such as the span of control and the chain of command as the business develops. You should also be aware of the effects of centralisation or decentralisation. You need to know about the different types of integration and be able to explain the reasons why businesses integrate, as well as the difference between mergers and takeovers or acquisitions.

Test yourself

Copy the table below and fit the following definitions of size into the spaces:

fewer than 50	£2m–8m	£8m+
250+	£1m–£3m	less than £1m
£3m+	50–249	less than £2m

	Employees	Revenue	Assets
Small			
Medium			
Large			

Try this

Question based on the 'Business and change' option

Merrion's Garage Services Ltd is a private limited company owned by John Merrion and his family. Due to its continuing success, Merrion's is thinking of expanding. The business could:
- acquire a rival garage
- diversify into other areas
- merge with a local car showroom

(a) Explain what is meant by 'diversify'. **(1 mark)**
(b) Explain the difference between a merger and an acquisition. **(2 marks)**
(c) Recommend one of the options to John Merrion, outlining your reasons. **(6 marks)**

Management styles

Core knowledge

Someone has to make the decisions within a business. What will the business produce and how many? Whom will it employ? What markets will it target? Making these decisions and, just as importantly, communicating them to people further down the business is the job of **managers**. The style that they choose to use will affect how efficiently the business operates and how well staff react to their decisions.

TOPFOTO

Richard Branson, head of Virgin, makes strategic decisions such as whether to run a railway. Operational decisions, such as where to seat people, may be made by train staff.

Speak the language

managers — the people who make decisions in a business

operational decisions — decisions about the day-to-day running of a business

strategic decisions — decisions about the general direction of a business

tactical decisions — decisions about intermediate targets and how they will be reached

What is management?

Managers make decisions, set targets and check progress. Top managers make **strategic decisions**. They have an overview and decide on the general direction of a business. Middle managers make **tactical decisions**. They decide on intermediate targets and how they will be reached. Other managers make **operational decisions**. These involve the day-to-day running of a business. In terms of staff, for instance, a strategic decision might be that the business should have more specialist staff, the tactical decision will be on where and when to hire them, and the operational decision will come down to things like hours of work and when holidays can be taken.

Motivation

The type of management is really important for a business. Employees work much better if they are motivated — that is, if they want to work. Giving employees a say in decision making is one way to motivate them. For this reason, many businesses include worker representatives on management boards.

Management styles

Managers can use a number of different styles of management. The most common of these are as follows:

- *Autocratic.* Managers make decisions on their own and tell others what to do. This has the advantage of showing clear leadership but may upset people.

- *Democratic*. Managers involve others in decision making. This helps people to feel involved but could lead to poor decisions.
- *Laissez-faire*. Managers allow subordinates to make their own decisions. This gives workers power, but can produce poor decisions.
- *Bureaucratic*. Managers follow the rulebook. This is inflexible, but everyone knows where they stand.

Which style?

The style adopted may depend on the situation and the decision being made. For example, to meet an order, a manager may have to say, 'I want it done this way, now'. On the other hand, if the business is deciding between several alternative new products, a manager might be better saying to a group, 'You decide, on the basis of your experience and a group view'. The first would be autocratic, the second laissez-faire (it's French for 'let it be'). The best managers adopt different styles to suit different situations.

Boost your grade

Remember that managers have to show leadership qualities in order for people to follow them. Before thinking about the type of management needed, think about the decision that is being made. Now decide whether it is urgent or must be done in a certain way, or whether other people could be involved in the decision about how to do it. You can then justify the management style chosen.

Key points

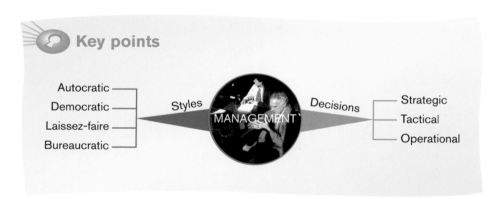

What does the specification require?

The specification covers management styles in the section on 'People in organisations'. You should be able to describe the different leadership styles that managers might have or can use, and be aware of the situations in which they might be appropriate. You need to know how these can be changed to be appropriate to the size, structure or objectives of a business, or to a particular situation in a business.

Test yourself

Match each term with its correct definition.

1 autocratic	**a** Managers follow the rulebook.
2 democratic	**b** Managers make decisions on their own and tell others what to do.
3 laissez-faire	**c** Managers involve others in decision making.
4 bureaucratic	**d** Managers allow subordinates to make their own decisions.

Try this

Core paper question

> Fiveways Farm Ltd is a large dairy farm. It produces milk, cream and cheese, and has recently gone into making bio-yoghurts. Dan Farrer owns Fiveways. The farm has recently grown and Dan has employed a manager, Asif, to help him run the business. Asif produces a daily list of tasks for each worker, and a system of records for workers to record when tasks are complete. The workers, however, are not consulted about the tasks. They are not used to this system and some have objected.

(a) Explain what management style Asif has adopted. **(2 marks)**

(b) Explain what disadvantages this style might bring. **(4 marks)**

Communication

Core knowledge

Clear communication is vital to all businesses. If the right message does not get to the right person, in the right format, then the business is failing to be efficient. Even worse, if the wrong messages are passed on, or in the wrong format, this could finish the business. Any communication consists of five parts:

The sender sends the message; the medium is text on the mobile phone; the feedback comes when the receiver responds and texts back

- the sender – the person or organisation sending the message
- the message – news, information, requests etc.
- the **medium** – the way the message is sent
- the receiver – the person or organisation to whom the message is addressed

- the feedback — the response to the message that lets the sender know it has been received

Types of message

Communications may be internal or external. Internal ones take place within the organisation. External ones take place with people or bodies outside the organisation. Businesses communicate with all their **stakeholders**. The types of medium used are both written and oral and include leaflets, catalogues, reports, press briefings, advertisements, formal documents, letters and meetings.

Formal communications

Formal communications have a set format and are used for certain types of message. Examples are a formal letter of appointment to a job or a formal meeting like the **AGM** of a business. With a formal message there is usually a set format (e.g. the layout of a business letter) and a record of the communication is kept (e.g. the minutes of a meeting). The main types of formal document are as follows:

- *Reports.* These might be aimed internally (e.g. on how well a department is doing) or externally (e.g. end-of-year company reports).
- *Letters.* These are usually written on headed note-paper and a copy kept on file for reference. They are used for official requests and notifications (e.g. an appointment or disciplinary action).

Documents are for formal communication

Key points

When sending a message, the sender should ask the following:

- Whom is this for?
- Does it need to be private?
- Does it need to be secure?
- Does a record need to be kept?
- Is a formal or informal approach appropriate?

Only then can the SENDER choose the right MEDIUM for the MESSAGE, so that the RECEIVER understands and can give FEED-BACK.

Boost your grade

The key to successful business communications is twofold. First, it is to make sure that the message is sent to the right person. Often messages fail because they have been sent to the wrong person and may not then be dealt with. Second, it is to make sure that the right medium is used. A formal communication requires a formal medium and specific documents (e.g. financial documents) may have been developed for specific purposes.

■ *Memoranda*. Usually shortened to 'memos', these are often written on headed paper to make them official.

■ *Forms*. Pre-printed and set-out forms ensure that important actions are carried out accurately and fairly.

Some face-to-face or oral communications also take place according to a set format. These include interviews, meetings, staff reviews and disciplinary actions.

Informal communications

Informal communications can take place at any time, using any medium. Sometimes these can be more powerful than formal communications. For example, if a teacher needed some boxes moving, which would be quicker — filling in an official request (formal) or having a quiet word with the caretaker (informal)?

What does the specification require?

'Communication in business activity' is a major part of the 'Business communication and marketing' option. You need to be able to explain the meaning and use of different types of communication (documentary, verbal, text and images, and one-way and two-way communication), and to understand the role that effective communication plays in the success of a business. You need to be aware of the barriers that can stand in the way of effective communication, such as timing, clarity, method used, attitude of receiver and sender, and appropriateness of feedback.

You should be able to quote specific examples — from a case study or your own knowledge — of how internal and external, formal and informal communication takes place, with a particular emphasis on developments in business communication and how these are having an impact on employment patterns. Areas such as home working, remote working or the movement of call centres abroad could all be studied.

Test yourself

Copy and complete the following sentences:

.... communications take place within a business. .... communications take place between businesses and other groups. They may be in a set format, called .... communications, or can take place outside a framework, called .... communications. The originator of communication is the ...., who sends the message through a particular way, or .... An important part of the process is that the .... provides .... to show that the message has been understood.

Try this

Question based on the 'Business communication and marketing' option

> PetsFirst sells a range of specialist pet foods and pet accessories via a mail order catalogue.
>
> The range of goods sold includes specialist food for dogs, cats and caged birds; toys for dogs and cats; cage toys for budgies; collars; and novelties with pet pictures, such as calendars, tea towels and place mats.
>
> The owners wanted to find out what other products existing customers might want, so they commissioned a telephone survey comprising 25 key questions. The call centre from which the survey was carried out was based in India and called customers between 7 p.m. and 8 p.m.

The survey showed a very poor response from customers and did not prove of any use to the business. Explain the reasons why this could have happened.

(4 marks)

The role of ICT

Core knowledge

ICT stands for information and communications technology. It is so vital to business that the government wants to make sure that everyone is trained in it. Therefore the subject is on all school timetables. There is also extra money available for people who want to train to be teachers of ICT. ICT is used for internal communication, within a business, and external communication, with other businesses and individuals.

Palmtops enable people to work wherever they are

Hardware

Hardware refers to communications equipment. This includes laptops, desktops, screens, projectors, servers and **peripherals** such as scanners and printers. Hardware is always improving – getting faster, smoother and capable of doing more complex tasks. For example, there are now palmtop devices that can take photographs and video, access the internet and send and receive e-mail (as well as being a mobile phone).

Software

Software refers to the **programs** run on computers. The most commonly used business programs are for:

The role of ICT

Speak the language

firewalls — protection of a network by setting up instructions that automatically block anything suspicious and only allow entry by password

peripherals — any hardware that is not part of a core computer system, but which may be added to it

programs — the sets of instructions that make a computer perform certain tasks; many are well-known commercial programs (US spelling is usual)

- word processing — creating documents, writing letters etc.
- spreadsheets — for mathematical tasks and to create graphs and charts
- databases — for managing lists and records that can be searched and sorted into different orders
- publishing (desk-top publishing or DTP — for the creation of professional-level publications)
- presentation — usually in the form of slides to which words, sound, pictures and movies can be added
- control technology — systems and devices that can be used to control events in production, check for quality, warn of problems etc. These include CAD (computer-aided design), CAM (computer-aided manufacture) and CIM (computer-integrated manufacture).

Networks

Networks internal to a business are called intranets. These are protected from outside access by passwords and other security features such as **firewalls**. Intranets may operate over several sites, which may even be in several countries. They can ensure that everyone in a large organisation gets the same messages at the same time.

The biggest external network is the internet. This is the collection of web pages that can be accessed via the world wide web. The internet makes finding information much easier.

ICT and the customer

A lot of ICT is now used at the point where a customer comes into contact with a business. This ranges from the use of bar code scanners and itemised bills at supermarket checkouts to personalised mailshots and e-mail enquiry services. ICT also provides the business with records of what customers have bought and can even update stock. It can improve customer service, provide extra services (such as online ordering or catalogues) and help a business to keep in closer touch with its customers.

Problems

ICT is not without its drawbacks:
- A computer is only as good as its operator, so if the wrong information is fed into it, then wrong information will come out. This is known as GIGO (garbage in, garbage out).
- Losing the personal touch — many customers (and employees) may feel that they no longer know the organisation.

- Speed of development. ICT moves on so fast that continual expenditure is needed to keep up.
- Viruses can destroy records and attack software. They mean that computers have to be protected.

Misuse of e-mail

One of the problems of some electronic media is that, although they are used for basically informal communications, a record is still kept. While a conversation criticising an organisation may go unnoticed, an e-mail or text may come to light. People may also send the wrong messages to the wrong people. For example, an internet 'joke' circulated 'to all' could offend some people and get the sender into trouble. Electronic media have made sending messages (particularly internationally) cheaper and more efficient, but they have many drawbacks regarding privacy, security and fitness for purpose.

Boost your grade

The most common answer that examiners see when they ask questions about the use of ICT is that it is 'quick and easy' and 'free and accurate'. You can gain higher marks by recognising that none of these is necessarily true. For ICT to be quick and accurate, a level of training and care needs to be built up over a number of years. This starts with young people in school and is therefore a long-term and costly exercise. Operators can also input incorrect information with disastrous results. The proper use of much software requires a high level of training.

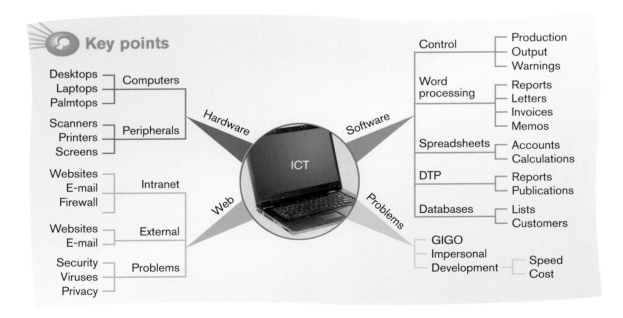

Key points

What does the specification require?

You should be able to comment on the ways in which ICT developments are having an impact on business and recruitment. Examples of developments are electronic data transmission, stock control systems, the development of regional distribution centres and online ordering. Possible impacts on business include changes in employment patterns, job losses and the advantages and disadvantages of technology to the efficiency of the business.

Test yourself

Match each item of software below to its correct function:

1 word processing	**a** systems and devices that can be used to control events in production, check for quality, warn of problems etc.
2 spreadsheet	**b** usually in the form of slides to which words, sound, pictures and movies can be added
3 database	**c** creating documents, writing letters etc.
4 publishing	**d** for the creation of professional-level publications
5 presentation	**e** for managing lists and records that can be searched and sorted into different orders
6 control technology	**f** for mathematical tasks and to create graphs and charts

Try this

Question based on the 'Business communication and marketing' option

PetsFirst sells a range of specialist pet foods and pet accessories via a mail order catalogue.

Suggest ways in which PetsFirst could improve efficiency through the use of ICT applications in three of the following areas:

- communication
- record keeping
- finance
- marketing

(6 marks)

Test on Chapter 3

1 Long-term goals of businesses are usually called:

A aims   D smart targets
B objectives   E progress points
C targets

2 Which of the following is **not** a major cause of business failure?

A no market for the product
B sales forecasts too optimistic
C not enough debt
D not enough money
E costs higher than anticipated

3 External stakeholders are likely to be:

A the owners of the business
B the community where the business operates
C employees of the business
D shareholders in the business
E managers of the business

4 The organisation of a large business is unlikely to be based on which of the following?

A product   D location
B function   E process
C agencies

5 The 'A' in 'SMART target' stands for:

A allowable   D achievable
B acceptable   E ample
C adequate

6 A mission statement is used by a business to:

A help customers choose products
B help show the aims of the business
C help shareholders see how well the business is doing
D help suppliers to see what the business wants
E fool competitors

7 A small business is generally defined as one with how many employees?

A up to 20   D up to 250
B up to 50   E over 250
C up to 100

8 A large business is generally defined as one with how much in assets?

A £1m+   D £4m+
B £2m+   E £5m+
C £3m+

9 A manager who follows the rulebook is generally called:

A autocratic   D laissez-faire
B bureaucratic   E strategic
C democratic

10 Which of the following refers to the way that a message is sent?

A sender   D receiver
B ICT   E feedback
C medium

Chapter 4
Finance

The finance function is central to all businesses. Before a business can begin trading, it needs finance to buy stock or equipment, to pay for premises and services, and to get in touch with customers and offer the product for sale. The finance function includes raising this initial money. It is also the job of finance to keep records of money in and money out and to advise management if there is likely to be a problem.

In a small business, these functions are often done by the owner, although an outside expert like an accountant may be brought in at key times during the year.

Once started, a business needs money to continue trading — for example, to advertise, pay bills or buy more stock. As a business becomes more successful, it may need to expand. As it continues to operate, equipment will wear out and need replacing. All these mean that further finance may be needed.

Sources of finance

Core knowledge

The money that a business needs may come from its owners, from lenders or people who are willing to take a risk, or from other outside sources. Usually there is a risk attached to borrowing money, but that is what enterprise is all about — risk taking.

Every business needs money

Owners' funds

One of the main sources of finance for starting a business is the money that the owners already have. They can risk this in the business in the hope that the business will be profitable. Sole traders may use their own funds. Partnerships will share resources. Limited companies can raise funds by selling shares to the owners (the shareholders). Once a business is a success and profitable, it may keep some of its profit for future finance. This is called **retained profit**.

Borrowing

If business owners do not already have the funds, then they need to borrow them. Usually businesses borrow from lending institutions such as banks. The most common forms of business borrowing are shown in the table below. There is a cost to borrowing. Usually this takes the form of interest. Generally, the riskier the loan and the longer the period of borrowing, the more interest will need to be paid.

Short-term (from a few days up to 3 years)	Medium-term (from 3 years to 10 years)	Long-term (10 years +)
Overdrafts	Hire purchase	Loans
Loans	Loans	Mortgages
Trade credit	Debentures	
Factoring		

The types of borrowing can be described as follows:

- *Trade credit* — a business promises to pay in the future for goods that it has received (hopefully, it will pay for the goods after it has sold them). The period of trade credit can be up to 90 days but is often less. Unusually, interest is seldom charged — but there will be penalties if payment is not made and there could be **discounts** for early payment.
- *Overdrafts* — a bank allows a business to take more out of its account than it has in, up to an agreed limit.

Speak the language

discount — a reduction in price

retained profit — amounts not distributed to owners but 'ploughed back' into the business

start-up grant — an initial sum of money, given to help a business become established

This is very flexible and interest is only charged on what is actually owed, for the time that it is owed.

- *Loans* — borrowing a fixed amount, for a fixed term. The business makes regular repayments and is charged interest on the full amount for the term of the loan.
- *Factoring* — selling debts to a specialist firm, which then collects the money owed. The factoring firm make its money by paying less for the debt than it actually collects.
- *Hire purchase* — paying for a piece of plant or equipment in instalments. The business can use the item while it is still paying for it.
- *Mortgages* — long-term loans used to buy expensive items such as land or buildings.
- *Debentures* — guarantees to pay at a time in the future, which may offer low risk but good interest rates for investors. They can be issued by large businesses.

Secured and unsecured borrowing

Banks can sell assets if a loan is secured

A mortgage is a secured loan; an overdraft is likely to be unsecured. But what does this mean? In the case of the mortgage, if it is not paid, the lending institution may be able to retrieve its money by seizing and selling the asset (a house or factory, for instance). If the loan is unsecured, the lender has no security of this type.

Grants

Sometimes businesses do not have to use their own funds or borrow them, because there are grants available. A grant is a sum of money made available to a business by a body such as central government, the European Union or a local council. Charities may also provide grants. The Prince's Youth Business Trust, for example, provides **start-up grants** for businesses set up by young people.

Key points

All businesses need finance. There are three main sources:

- owners' own money — owners' funds
- money from banks or other lenders — borrowed funds
- money that does not have to be repaid — grants

Boost your grade

Sometimes private speculators want to help businesses by letting them have money. They may do this in return for a share of the profits in a business, or for partial control. Such people are called venture capitalists. They provide the capital, but obviously at a risk of losing their money. Often the businesses that they back are involved in exciting developments or cutting-edge technology that other lending institutions are not keen on. The venture capitalists take the risk, but hope for excitement and a big reward.

What does the specification require?

Accounting and finance is studied in several parts of the core specification. It appears in section on 'External environment of business'. It is therefore looked at in the context of how businesses use finance and accounting tools to help them to make decisions, and is flagged as 'Financing business activity'. In 'Business structure, organisation and control', the section on 'Financing business activity' asks you to understand the needs of the business for finance and the various sources of finance. In the section on 'Business behaviour', the heading is 'Financial information and decision making'. This section focuses on financial tools such as forecasts and financial accounts. The optional area 'Business and change' has a section on 'Finance and change' that covers similar ground, but in more detail.

In the context of this section, you need to know the difference between short- and long-term finance in terms of where it comes from, what it costs and why each might be needed by a particular business. You should be able to identify both internal and external sources of finance for private- and public-sector organisations. In particular, you should be able to comment on the factors that affect the methods of finance chosen by a particular business, such as the nature of the business or proposed project, the size and/or structure of the business, and the cost of the finance related to risk, source and length of borrowing time.

Test yourself

Organise the following forms of finance under the headings short term, medium term and long term (some may go into more than one category):

➤ debentures ➤ overdrafts ➤ loans ➤ factoring
➤ trade credit ➤ hire purchase ➤ mortgages

Try this

Question based on the 'Business and change' option

Merrion's Garage Services Ltd is a private limited company owned by John Merrion and his family. When the company was established, John had three main sources of finance to pay the set-up costs. These were:

■ owners' funds ■ bank loan ■ overdraft

(a) Explain what is meant by each of these. **(6 marks)**
(b) Explain why John might have needed more than one source of finance. **(4 marks)**

Costs and revenue

Core knowledge

Businesses produce either a good for sale or a service. If it is a good, there are raw materials and other inputs to pay for. If it is a service, the business needs to let people know that it exists. In either case, therefore, there are costs. The money that the business receives for its sales is called revenue. Business costs are divided into fixed costs — also called indirect costs or **overheads** — and variable costs.

A café needs to buy tables and chairs, crockery and cutlery, as well as stock, before it can start trading. It then has to pay for power, wages, cleaning and more stock to stay operational

Fixed costs

Fixed costs do not vary with **output** — that is, with the amount produced. Examples are rent, interest payments and rates. They have to be paid whether or not a business is producing.

Variable costs

Variable costs are those costs that vary with output, such as raw materials, packaging, parts and components, ingredients, power and labour charges. Total cost is fixed cost plus variable cost. Sometimes it is difficult to decide whether a cost is fixed or variable, as it may have elements of both within it. **Utilities** are a case in point. A power or telecommunications bill, for example, has a fixed element for the supply of the service, plus a variable element for the amount of the service used.

Semi-variable costs

These are costs that do vary with output, but not directly. For example, a business may need to pay overtime, or a shop may need to open for longer hours.

Other definitions

Costs can be divided into start-up costs and running costs. Start-up costs are only paid when setting up a business. Financing this may become part of a business's fixed costs. Running or operational costs have to be paid to keep the business going. These may be fixed costs such as rent, or variable costs such as wages.

Boost your grade

Don't fall into the trap of giving incorrect definitions. Remember that fixed costs are *not* costs that 'do not vary' (a common mistake), but ones that 'do not vary *with output*'.

Key points

- Fixed costs do not vary with output.
- Variable costs vary with output.
- Semi-variable costs vary indirectly with output.
- Start-up costs are paid to get a business started.
- Running costs are paid to keep it going.

What does the specification require?

You need to be able to classify the costs of a business and compare costs with revenue to determine profit (or loss) in a business context. According to the 'Financing business activity' section of the specification, you need to understand the use and management of finance. This includes the capitalisation of a company, an analysis of its balance sheet and how this forecasts cash flow.

Test yourself

1 Fixed costs are costs that:

  A do not change

  B change with output

  C do not change with output

  D always stay the same

2 Which of the following is most likely to be an example of a variable cost?

  A rent

  B rates

  C interest payments

  D raw materials

3 Another name for fixed costs is:

  A underheads

  B overheads

  C raw materials

  D labour costs

4 Revenue is defined as:

  A price × number sold

  B price × fixed costs

  C price × variable costs

  D fixed costs × variable costs

5 The one-off costs paid to set up a business are called:

  A operational costs

  B running costs

  C fixed costs

  D start-up costs

Try this

Question based on the 'Business and change' option

> Merrion's Garage Services Ltd is a private limited company owned by John Merrion and his family. The garage has a scale of charges as shown below.
>
> | | |
> |---|---|
> | Standard service | £50.00 |
> | Wash and valet | £12.00 |
> | Deluxe service (includes wash and valet) | £60.00 |

Last month the business carried out 40 standard services, 118 wash and valets and 132 deluxe services. Calculate last month's total revenue from the three services. Show your working.

(3 marks)

Breaking even

Core knowledge

When revenue is greater than costs, a business is making a profit. When revenue is less than costs, the business is making a loss. The point where the amount of revenue is equal to the amount of costs is called the **breakeven point**. At this point the business is making neither a profit nor a loss.

Breakeven charts

Breakeven can be simplified by assuming that the fixed and variable costs of a business, along with its revenue, can be accurately measured. This can then be shown in a table.

Number sold	Sales revenue (£)	Fixed costs (£)	Variable costs (£)	Total costs (£)
0	0	15	0	15
1	10	15	5	20
2	20	15	10	25
3	30	15	15	30
4	40	15	20	35
5	50	15	25	40

This business is selling items priced at £10. Sales revenue is therefore this price times the number sold. Fixed costs do not change as output changes, so these are shown as a constant £15. Variable costs (e.g. raw materials) do change as output changes. They are therefore shown as rising in units of £5 as output rises. Adding fixed costs to variable costs gives total costs. The point where total costs are equal to total revenue is the breakeven point — at sales of 3 units, as highlighted in the table.

At lower sales levels, total costs are higher than total revenue, so the business is making a loss. At higher sales levels, total costs are lower than total revenue, so the business is making a profit.

Breakeven graphs

Breakeven can also be shown in graph form. The point where the total costs line crosses total revenue is breakeven. Fewer sales (red) mean a loss; more sales (yellow) mean a profit. The further away sales are from the breakeven point, the greater the profit or loss.

Moving breakeven

If a business is making a loss, it can try to make changes. It can seek either to lower costs or to increase revenue. Managers can use breakeven as a tool to help them predict what might happen as a result of such changes.

Contribution

The example we have been looking at assumes a single product, and that all output is sold. Obviously this is not always the case. To see how each product is doing, managers can use the **contribution** method. This looks at the contribution to overall revenue from the sale of each product. Contribution is calculated by taking the variable costs of a product away from its revenue. The formula for working out the number of sales necessary to break even is then:

$$\text{breakeven sales} = \frac{\text{fixed costs}}{\text{contribution}}$$

It is also important for a business to look at revenue — that is, actual sales — rather than the number produced, as some products may not be sold.

Speak the language

breakeven — the point where a business is making neither profit nor loss

contribution — a method of using breakeven to show how much (if anything) each product contributes to profit

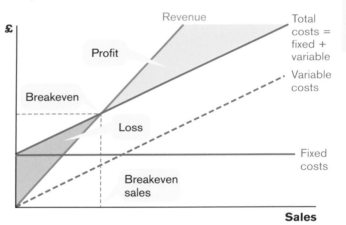

Which item is contributing profit; which is making a loss?

Key points

At one level, in theory, breakeven is very easy. Does revenue cover costs? At another level, it can be very difficult and of little use to a business that produces multiple products and sells them in many markets. Contribution can give an idea of how important each product is to the business, but it can be difficult to allocate costs and make this accurate.

Boost your grade

Breakeven charts and graphs can be used to carry out 'what if' questions. 'What if sales fell?' 'What if the price of raw materials rose?' You should always take such questions past the first stage to see what other consequences there might be. For example, if there were a rise in costs, the business might feel that it has to raise prices to increase revenue. However, increased prices might lead to fewer sales and lower revenue.

What does the specification require?

Under 'Finance and change' in the 'Business and change' option, you need to be able to explain and illustrate how costs change with output. You should be able to define fixed and variable costs and say what effect economies of scale might have on them. You should also be able to define revenue so that you can work out a breakeven point. You should be able to draw a breakeven graph and show, using the graph, what changes might be made to costs, prices, output or sales in order to manage breakeven.

Test yourself

Copy the graph below and add the correct labels.

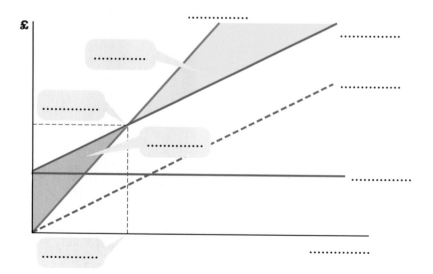

Core paper question

> Sarah has set up a hairdressing business. She wanted to know how many standard cut and blow-dries she would have to sell in order to break even. She found that her fixed costs in the first year would be £20,000. The variable cost per cut and blow-dry is £15 and she intends to price them at £25 each.

(a) Suggest one fixed cost and one variable cost that Sarah must pay.

(2 marks)

(b) Calculate Sarah's breakeven in the first year of operation. Show your working.

(8 marks)

Financial documents

Core knowledge

Think about a transaction that you have carried out in a shop. What paperwork was involved? What about if you ordered something online? When you buy something in a shop you are entitled to a receipt, to show that you have paid for the goods. The business also keeps a record of the purchase.

Business-to-consumer transactions (B2C)

The process of ordering, buying and paying for something involves records. Imagine buying a present from a catalogue. You order it, it is delivered with a request for payment, you pay for it. Buying from the internet is similar. You order the good, usually pay for it then and there, and receive a receipt to print off. The business then delivers it. If you are unhappy with it, you can return it and get a refund.

Business-to-business transactions (B2B)

Business-to-business transactions are not much different. If a business wants to buy something, say stock for sale or raw materials, it will buy it from another business. There are three phases to the transaction: the order, the delivery and the payment. Each has its own special document to make sure that each business has a record of the **transaction**.

A till receipt is a familiar financial document

The order

Another word for 'buy' is 'purchase'. Businesses use a *purchase order* to say what they want to buy, how much they want and what they expect to pay. Between businesses, it is rare for payment to be made at this stage. Usually it is made on delivery.

The delivery

The goods are delivered to the buyer, who signs the *delivery note* to show that the goods have been accepted. The buyer completes its own paperwork to show that the goods have been received. This *goods received note* is passed to finance so that it knows it can pay for the goods.

The payment

The seller prepares a bill for the buyer, so that it knows how much to pay, when and how. This is called a *sales invoice*. This will match the description of the goods delivered on the delivery note. The buyer then pays for the goods. Another word for payment is 'remittance'. A *remittance advice* slip is sent with the payment. This says what the money is for. The seller may then send the buyer a *receipt*, to show that payment has been accepted. If an order is incomplete or there is a problem with it, the seller may issue a *credit note*, allowing the buyer credit against a future purchase.

Regular business

If the two businesses trade together regularly, the buyer may have an account with the seller. In this case, the buyer may be invoiced on a regular basis. A record of sales and payments will be kept on a statement of account, prepared by the seller and checked by the buyer.

What does the specification require?

The flow of financial documents is not specifically examined, although they could be studied within the 'Communications in business activity' option or to illustrate the different stakeholders in an organisation.

Test yourself

Copy and complete the following sentences:

Businesses use a .... to say what they want to buy, how much they want and what they expect to pay. The goods are delivered to the buyer, who signs the .... to show that the goods have been accepted. The buyer completes a .... to show that the goods have been received. The .... shows the buyer how much to pay, when and how. The seller may then send the buyer a .... to show that payment has been accepted.

Try this

Core paper question

Sarah is setting up a hairdressing business. She has written a business plan to present to her bank manager in order to raise a loan for the business.

Outline the major areas that Sarah should cover in this document.   **(8 marks)**

The balance sheet

Core knowledge

Businesses need to know how much they are worth. To find out, a business can use its balance sheet. This shows it how much it owns against how much it owes. The balance sheet is often called a 'snapshot' because it shows the situation at the point at which it was drawn up. The balance sheet for a small business is relatively simple; that for a larger business more complex, but the principles are the same.

CAROL BUCHANAN/ALAMY

What is in balance?

The balance sheet is called a 'balance' because what the business owns and what it owes must

What's it all worth?

The balance sheet

Sample balance sheet

ASSETS	£000	TOTAL £000
Fixed		
Factory	1,000	
Vehicles	800	
Furniture	200	2,000
Current		
Stock	700	
Debtors (owe money)	200	
Cash	100	1,000
		3,000
CURRENT LIABILITIES		
Creditors	500	
Overdraft	500	1,000
Net current assets		
(total assets less current liabilities)		2,000
minus Long-term liabilities		500
Net assets employed		
(what the business is worth)		1,500
CAPITAL		
Shares issued	500	
Reserves	500	
Profit	500	1,500

be equal. Essentially, both sides of the balance are measuring the same things. Think about what you own and owe. These are your assets and liabilities. The amount borrowed or earned to buy the assets must equal what you paid for them. If you deduct your liabilities from your assets, you know how much you are worth. It is the same with a business.

The account

There are three parts to a balance sheet. Each is linked to the others. They are:

- **assets** — what a business owns
- **liabilities** — what a business owes
- **capital** — where the business has raised its money from

Assets

Items are only assets if they can be valued. 'Reputation', for example, does not appear in a balance sheet. Assets are either *fixed* (e.g. buildings and machinery used in production) or *current* (e.g. stocks of finished product that could be easily turned into cash, or money that is owed to the business by **debtors**).

Liabilities

Items are only liabilities if they can be valued. Liabilities are either *current* (debts that must be paid back within a year, such as bank overdrafts and debts owed to **creditors**) or *long term* (debts that the business has more than a year to repay, such as long-term loans and mortgages).

What's it worth?

Take the liabilities away from the assets and what is left is what the business is worth. This is called *net assets employed*.

Capital

The final part of the account shows how the money for these net assets employed was raised. This could be via shares, through profit, or from profit made in previous periods (reserves). Capital must balance with net current assets.

Speak the language

assets — anything that a business owns that has a value

creditors — those to whom the business owes money, such as banks

debtors — those who owe the business money, such as other businesses that have yet to pay for goods bought

liabilities — anything that a business owes that has a value

Key points

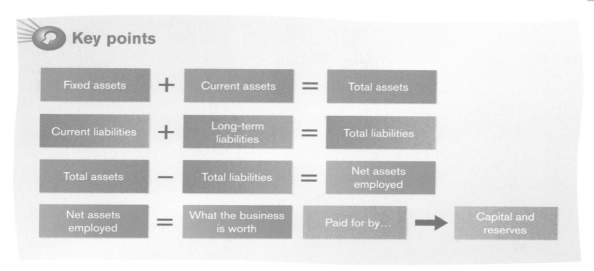

What does the specification require?

You may need to interpret part of the final accounts of a business. To do this, you should know how a balance sheet is put together (and why) and suggest (using the figures) possible directions or policies for a business. The focus in OCR is on using financial tools such as the balance sheet to aid decision making. You could, for instance, be asked to give advice to a case study business.

Boost your grade

Don't worry too much about the various parts of the balance sheet. If you remember that it is a snapshot of what the business owns (assets) set against what the business owes (liabilities) and that liabilities are always taken away from assets, this should be enough for you to complete an example, if this is what is required. The balance sheet *must balance*.

Test yourself

Decide whether each of the following is an asset or liability.
- Cash in hand
- Cash in the bank
- Creditors
- Debtors
- Factory
- Furniture
- Machinery
- Overdraft
- Stock
- Vehicles

Try this

Core paper question

Fiveways Farm Ltd is a large dairy farm. It produces milk, cream and cheese, and has recently gone into making bio-yoghurts.

Extract from the balance sheet of Fiveways Farm Ltd (£)

Year	2007	2006	2005
Fixed assets	250,000	240,000	235,000
Current assets	270,000	260,000	245,000
Current liabilities	90,000	85,000	75,000
Net current assets	180,000	175,000	170,000

(a) Calculate the increase in Fiveways Farm's total assets between 2005 and 2007. Show your working.

(3 marks)

(b) Explain possible reasons why Fiveways Farm's fixed assets have increased over this period.

(3 marks)

Profit and loss account

Core knowledge

One of the usual aims of a business is to make a **profit** and to avoid making a **loss**: in other words, to take in more in revenue than is spent in costs. The profit and loss account looks back over the previous year's performance to see how well the business is doing. The information can then be used to compare this year with previous years (is it doing better or worse?) and to help plan for the future. Sole traders and other small businesses keep fairly simple accounts. The accounts of limited companies are more complex but the principles are the same.

Sample profit and loss account

TRADING ACCOUNT			£000	£000
Sales revenue				5,000
minus Cost of sales	Opening stock	1,000		
	plus Purchases	2,000		
	less Closing stock	500	2,500	
Gross profit				2,500
PROFIT AND LOSS ACCOUNT				
Gross profit				2,500
minus Expenses	Rent	250		
	Wages	250		
	Transport	200		
	Power	100		
	Equipment	200	1,000	
Net profit				1,500
APPROPRIATION ACCOUNT				
Net profit				1,500
minus Taxation				500
Profit after taxation				1,000
minus Dividends paid				500
Retained profit				500

The account

There are three parts to the profit and loss account:

- trading account – what the business has sold and what it has cost to achieve these sales
- profit and loss account – gross profit minus expenses
- appropriation account – where the net profit has gone

Income

The account shows what the business has earned. This is called its income. The biggest source of income for most businesses is sales revenue. However, the cost of buying or making the items sold has to be deducted from this total. This is called 'cost of sales'. If you buy 10 pencils at 8p each and sell them at 10p each, your revenue is 10 × 10p = £1, but the cost of sales is 10 × 8p = 80p. Your gross profit is thus 20p.

Stock
The only time this is different is if you have stock left over. This is your 'opening stock' for the next year. If you only sell 9 pencils, your revenue is 90p, the cost of sales is still 80p and gross profit is 10p, but you have one pencil in stock to start the next year.

Expenses
Buying and selling the pencils will have taken you time; you may also need somewhere to sell them from. These are all expenses. A bigger business will have to pay items like wages, rent on premises, power bills and equipment costs.

Gross and net profit
Gross profit is the amount that you have made before expenses are taken into account. Net profit is the amount after expenses are deducted.

Appropriation account
The third part of the profit and loss account shows what happens to the gross profit. This is called the appropriation account. Some of it goes in taxes, some may be given to shareholders in the form of dividends and some may be kept to help the finances of the business.

> **Speak the language**
>
> loss — costs are greater than revenue
>
> profit — revenue is greater than costs

> **Boost your grade**
>
> Gross profit and net profit are usually included only once in an account. Gross profit links the trading account to the profit and loss account. Net profit links the profit and loss account to the appropriation account.

Key points

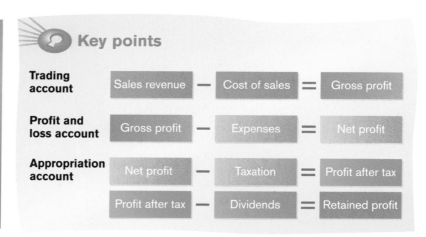

Trading account: Sales revenue − Cost of sales = Gross profit

Profit and loss account: Gross profit − Expenses = Net profit

Appropriation account: Net profit − Taxation = Profit after tax

Profit after tax − Dividends = Retained profit

What does the specification require?

You need to be able to define profit (and loss) and to explain the importance of profit as a reward for enterprise and risk taking, financing further investment and indicating business performance. You should also show that you understand the main parts of a profit and loss account. You need to be able to carry out calculations as well as providing definitions. You should be able to calculate gross and net profit, and use the calculations in given situations to support business decision making.

For the 'Finance and change' part of the 'Business and change' option, you will need to classify and give examples of fixed and current assets, current and long-term liability, and the types of capital used in business organisations. You will lose marks if you do not use '£' signs and either '000s' or 'millions' where appropriate. You should always show your working in numerical questions.

Test yourself

Copy and complete the account, deleting the alternatives (plus/minus, profit/ loss) that do not apply.

Trading account		£000	£000
Sales revenue			20,000
plus/minus Cost of sales	Opening stock	12,000	
	plus/minus Purchases	5,500	
	plus/minus Closing stock	2,000	....
Gross profit			....
plus/minus Expenses	Rent	500	
	Wages	2,000	
	Transport	750	
	Power	500	
	Equipment	500	....
Net profit/loss			....

The amount of profit/loss is therefore £ ....

Try this

Core paper question

Sarah's hairdressing business has now been running for 2 years. She has drawn up the profit and loss account for the previous year's trading, part of which is shown here.

Trading account: Sarah's Hairdressing

		£	£
Sales revenue from hairdressing and product sales			21,000
Minus cost of sales	Opening stock	18,500	
	Plus purchases	5,500	
	Less closing stock	8,000	16,000
Gross profit			**5,000**
Minus expenses	Rent	1,500	
	Wages	2,000	
	Transport	200	
	Power	500	
	Equipment	500	4,700
Net profit			**300**

(a) Explain whether or not Sarah is making a satisfactory level of net and gross profit. **(4 marks)**

(b) Suggest ways in which she could improve profitability. **(6 marks)**

Cash and cash flow

Core knowledge

A business has a constant flow of cash in and cash out. Cash comes in through sales revenue and flows out to pay for costs. It can take the form of bank transfers, cheques and credit or debit card transactions. A business needs enough cash to meet its day-to-day needs. The problem is that the flows of cash into and out of a business are never equal, so businesses need to manage these cash flows.

Cash flow

If there is more cash coming in than the business needs, this is called a *cash surplus*. If there is less cash than it needs, this is called a *cash shortage*. One of the major reasons why businesses go bust is cash shortages. Even if a business has full order books and is making a profit, it cannot survive if it cannot pay its immediate bills. This is often called a **cash-flow crisis**. Remember that it can be just as bad to have too much cash as to have too little. It is inefficient to have too much. It is better to turn an excess of cash into assets that can earn more money.

Forecasting

To avoid such problems, a business needs to **forecast** how much cash it will need. It can then budget carefully to make sure that it can always cover cash shortages. A cash-flow forecast is made from week to week or month to month. A typical 6-month forecast could look like this:

	Jan	Feb	Mar	Apr	May	June
Cash brought forward	1,000	1,000	1,000	1,000	1,000	1,000
+ Cash from sales	5,000	5,000	5,000	5,000	5,000	5,000
= Total cash available	6,000	6,000	6,000	6,000	6,000	6,000
− Cash out	5,000	5,000	5,000	5,000	5,000	5,000
= Cash to carry forward	1,000	1,000	1,000	1,000	1,000	1,000

However, flows are not usually as steady as this. By looking at last year's figures, the business might know that February and March are poor months for sales, but months in which costs are lower; that April is when the tax bill has to be settled; and that May is a bumper month. The forecast might then look like this:

	Jan	Feb	Mar	Apr	May	June
Cash brought forward	1,000	1,000	−1,000	−2,000	−5,000	3,000
+ Cash from sales	5,000	1,000	2,000	5,000	12,000	8,000
= Total cash available	6,000	2,000	1,000	3,000	7,000	11,000
− Cash out	5,000	3,000	3,000	8,000	4,000	4,000
= Cash to carry forward	1,000	1,000	−2,000	−5,000	3,000	7,000

The business can now plan what it needs to borrow and when. It knows that in April it will need an overdraft of £5,000. If its overdraft limit were £6,000, it would be very close to a cash-flow crisis. Note that this does not mean the business is doing badly — you can see that cash flow improves in later months.

The table can also be shown as a graph, usually a bar chart. The second table would show a cash flow like the one shown here.

Accuracy

Businesses can make their cash-flow forecasts more accurate by adding in details of where money is coming from and where it is going to. Cash in, for instance, could be broken down into cash from sales of different goods; cash out could be broken down to show how much is spent on items such as wages, taxation, power and stock. The forecast can be used to put together a **budget** so that a crisis point is not reached.

Visuals

A common way to think of cash flow is as the water running into a sink with the plug out. The flow from the taps represents cash in, while the flow through the plughole represents cash out. You can see that if one flow is greater than the other, the business (sink) will soon have too much or too little cash (water).

Key points

Cash is vital. Businesses need enough cash to pay bills. If a business knows when it is going to need cash it can plan to do something about it. It can:

- borrow money
- try to increase sales
- try to reduce costs
- spread costs more evenly (paying by instalment, for example)
- persuade people to pay more quickly

What does the specification require?

As with other financial tools, the focus of the specification is on how the business would use cash-flow forecasts to aid its decision making. A key area that you need to understand is the difference between profit and loss and cash flow — in particular, how a business that may be profitable can still find itself in trouble because it has not managed cash flow efficiently. You need to be aware, therefore, of the importance of cash flow and cash-flow forecasting. You need to be able to put a cash-flow forecast together and explain how it might be used.

In the 'Finance and change' part of the 'Business and change' option, you need to look at budgeting and to be able to explain why firms budget.

Test yourself

Choose three different businesses — for example, a sole trading hairdresser business, a limited company involved in manufacturing, and a plc supermarket chain. For each say what are the main inflows and the main outflows.

Try this

Coursework alternative paper question

Cash-flow forecast for Schwitt plc for the last 6 months of 2007 (£000)		July	Aug	Sept	Oct	Nov	Dec
Receipts	Revenue from sales	90	80	75	65	80	160
Payments	Wages and salaries	20	20	20	20	20	20
	Materials	20	20	20	20	30	30
	Power and maintenance	10	5	5	10	10	10
	Rent	20	20	20	20	20	20
	Transport	10	10	5	5	5	10
	Advertising	15	10	10	5	10	30
Total payments		95	85	80	80	95	120
Net cash flow		−5	−5	−5	−15	−15	40
Opening balance		25	20	15	10	−5	−20
Closing balance		20	15	10	−5	−20	20

Explain what happened to the company's cash-flow position in November 2007.

(8 marks)

Understanding and using ratios

Core knowledge

A ratio is one thing measured in terms of another. Ratios are very important in business. For example, a business needs to know how much profit it is making in terms of sales (profitability); how much profit it is making in terms of the capital invested; and how capable it is of paying its debts. There are ratios to measure all of these.

Profitability ratios

Profitability ratios measure how much profit a business is making compared with its revenue. Businesses look at the gross profit to revenue ratio and at the net profit to revenue ratio. These ratios use figures from the profit and loss account. For example, a business making £10,000 gross profit on £15,000 of sales is achieving a gross profit to revenue ratio of:

10,000:15,000 or 1:1.5

(10,000/15,000) × 100 = 66.66%

This is also called the **profit margin**. This business is making £66.66 gross profit for every £100 of sales.

A more important figure is net profit — the amount of profit left after expenses are taken off. Assuming this business had expenses of £8,000, the net profit to sales revenue would be:

2,000:15,000 or 2:15

(2,000/15,000) × 100 = 13.3%

Percentages

You can see from the above example why percentages are used. It is much easier to compare the two percentage figures than the two reduced ratios.

A net profit margin of 13.3% can be compared with the gross profit margin and with margins from previous years.

Liquidity

Liquidity is the term used to show how close an asset is to cash — in other words, how easily it can be turned into cash. Cash is the most liquid asset; stock is less liquid, but easily turned into cash if sold; a factory or plant is the least liquid.

Current ratio

Liquidity ratios look at how easily a business can pay its short-term debts from its assets. These figures are taken from the balance sheet. Current assets are divided by current liabilities to give the **current ratio**. A business with current assets of £20,000 and current liabilities of £5,000 would have a current ratio of:

20,000/5,000:1 = 4:1

The business can cover its debts four times over — a very healthy position. In general, a current ratio of between 1.5:1 and 3:1 is considered healthy. However, a ratio of 4:1 means the business is not making efficient use of its assets.

Acid test ratio

For many businesses, a large part of current assets will be stock waiting to be sold. If these sales do not happen, stock has to be taken out of the equation. If the business in our example had £16,000 worth of stock, then:

(20,000 − 16,000)/5,000:1
reduces to 4/5:1 or 0.8:1

To find the acid test ratio, stock has to be deducted from current sales

This 0.8:1 means that the business has just 80p with which to pay every £1 of short-term debt unless it sells some stock. This is called the **acid test ratio** and measures the real ability of a business to pay its debts. In general, an acid test ratio of between 1.5:1 and 3:1 is considered healthy. This business is carrying too much of its assets in stock.

Return on capital employed

ROCE is calculated by dividing net profit by total capital employed and expressing this as a percentage. It shows the ability of a business to make a profit from the capital invested in it.

Using ratios

While it is easy to work out ratios, it is more important to make sure that they are properly

interpreted. From year to year, they can be used to compare how well a business is doing. In any one year, they can show whether the business is in a strong or weak position.

Boost your grade

If you have the profit and loss account for a business, you can work out gross and net profit ratios and give an informed opinion on how profitable you think the business is. If you have the balance sheet of a business, you can work out how capable the business is of paying its debts and, again, give an informed opinion of how well you think the business is doing. To earn higher marks you must always have evidence to back your opinions and conclusions.

Key points

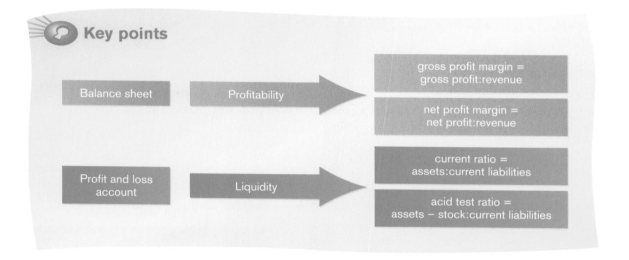

Balance sheet → Profitability →

gross profit margin = gross profit:revenue

net profit margin = net profit:revenue

Profit and loss account → Liquidity →

current ratio = assets:current liabilities

acid test ratio = assets − stock:current liabilities

What does the specification require?

Ratios are only covered in any detail in the 'Finance and change' part of 'Business and change', although you can bring them into other answers if it helps to show your knowledge or would support the decision making of the business. In 'Finance and change' you need to identify, interpret and comment on changes in business revealed by financial data in the various parts of company accounts, using tools such as ratios, trends and forecasts, and by making comparisons between accounts.

You must always make sure, with figures such as these, that you are comparing like with like — the axes on graphs or headings and units on tables will not always be directly comparable, so look out for this.

Test yourself

Write down the correct formulae for:

➤ gross profit to sales ratio
➤ net profit to sales ratio

➤ current ratio
➤ acid test ratio

Try this

Question based on the 'Business and change' option

Merrion's Garage Services Ltd is a private limited company owned by John Merrion and his family. The following is an extract from Merrion's 2007 trading account.

Trading account: Merrion's Garage Services Ltd (£)

	2007	2006
Sales revenue	40,000	30,000
Cost of sales	22,000	15,000
Gross profit	18,000	15,000
Profit and loss account		
Gross profit	18,000	15,000
Expenses	11,000	5,000
Net profit	7,000	5,000

(a) Suggest two items that might be included under 'Expenses'. **(2 marks)**

(b) Use the following ratios to explain whether the business was more or less profitable in 2007 than in 2006:

$$\text{gross profit to sales ratio} = \frac{\text{gross profit}}{\text{sales revenue}} \times 100$$

$$\text{net profit to sales ratio} = \frac{\text{net profit}}{\text{sales revenue}} \times 100$$

(8 marks)

Test on Chapter 4

1 Fixed costs are costs that:

A do not change
B change with output
C do not change with output
D always stay the same
E do not change very much

2 Revenue is defined as:

A price × number sold
B price × fixed costs
C price × variable costs
D fixed costs × variable costs
E fixed costs + variable costs

Test on Chapter 4

3 An example of a short-term form of finance is:

A hire purchase   D overdrafts
B loans   E trade credit
C mortgages

4 An example of a long-term form of finance is:

A hire purchase   D overdrafts
B loans   E trade credit
C mortgages

5 Which of the following is most likely to be an example of a variable cost?

A rent   D raw materials
B rates   E wages
C interest payments

6 The breakeven sales point is the point at which:

A sales are made   D a loss is made
B revenue is made   E neither profit nor
C a profit is made   loss is made

7 Which document is used to request payment from a business?

A receipt   D invoice
B delivery note   E goods received
C statement of   note
account

8 Which of the following is an example of a business's liability?

A cash in the bank   D factory
B creditors   E machinery
C debtors

9 Assets and liabilities are usually expressed in which financial format?

A breakeven chart
B balance sheet
C cash-flow forecast
D profit and loss account
E statement of account

10 Which financial format would usually include 'expenses'?

A breakeven chart
B balance sheet
C cash-flow forecast
D profit and loss account
E statement of account

11 Which financial format would usually include a prediction of borrowing requirements?

A breakeven chart
B balance sheet
C cash-flow forecast
D profit and loss account
E statement of account

12 The correct formula for net profit ratio is:

A $\frac{turnover}{sales} \times 100$ D $\frac{sales}{gross\ profit} \times 100$

B $\frac{gross\ profit}{sales}$ E $\frac{gross\ profit}{sales} \times 100$

C $\frac{net\ profit}{sales} \times 100$

13 Which of the following is least likely to be a suitable source of finance for a sole trader?

A share issue   D owners' funds
B bank loan   E trade credit
C overdraft

14 Which of the following would be considered a fixed cost?

A raw materials   D interest on a loan
B fuel   E cost of phone
C power   calls

15 The trading account is included as part of which of the following?

A breakeven chart
B balance sheet
C cash-flow forecast
D profit and loss account
E statement of account

Chapter 5
Human resources

The human resources function is responsible for staff. The usual 'life story' of an employee involves recruitment, training and retirement. Human resources is also responsible for discipline, including sacking staff if they break the rules. Another key responsibility of human resources is the motivation of workers.

Even if there are no staff, such as in a sole trader business, the owner still has to consider his or her own pay and conditions, and own training and development requirements. One of the key areas that a sole trader (or other small business) needs to consider is providing for retirement. Pensions, including personal pensions, have become a big issue for the government and for businesses. This is an area that may well turn up in future examination papers.

Pay and benefits

Core knowledge

Payment for work is usually in money, but it can be in other forms, such as **discounts** or 'perks' (e.g. company cars). A business wants workers who will do a fair day's work for a fair day's pay. Workers want to be paid fairly for the work they do.

Wages

The most common way for a business to pay its workers is through a **wage**. This is paid at regular intervals, usually weekly, and can be based on:
- time rates — pay linked to the number of hours worked

Speak the language

discount — a reduction in price, usually a percentage

motivate — to persuade workers to work harder because they want to

salary — an annual amount of pay, usually paid in 12 equal instalments

wage — a weekly payment for hours worked or work completed

The most common 'perk' is a company car

- piece rates — pay linked to the number of 'pieces' finished; that is, according to how much work has been done
- contract rates — pay made on the completion of a particular job; for example, the building of a house extension

Overtime is an extra payment made for working outside usual hours. It is generally paid at either 1.5 or 2 times normal pay.

Salaries

Salaries are usually quoted as an amount per year. A **salary** is normally paid in 12 monthly instalments. Overtime is not available for salaried workers — they are expected to do whatever is necessary to carry out the job and, to an extent, may be expected to manage their own time.

Perks

Businesses can decide to pay workers in other ways. 'Perks' are additional benefits that come with a job and form part of the pay package. For example, a worker at a travel agents may receive cheap holidays, airline staff are entitled to certain flights, retail assistants can usually buy discounted goods and bank staff may be allowed cheap loans or mortgages.

Profit sharing

One way to pay workers extra is by letting them share in the profits of the business. This also helps to **motivate** workers. If they are efficient and the business makes a profit, the workers gain more. Workers may also be paid with shares in the business. Again, as part owners, they should be better motivated to make the business a success.

How much is a job worth?

The general level of pay for a job is decided by a number of factors. These include the following:

- *Education.* Jobs that require higher levels of education usually offer higher pay rates.
- *Training.* If skills need to be learned or practised, this increases pay.
- *Unique skills.* If skills are in short supply, high pay may be demanded. In this category are professional footballers and entertainers.
- *Conditions.* People who work in uncomfortable or dangerous professions expect to be paid to compensate them for this.

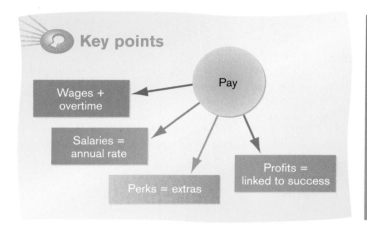

Key points

Wages + overtime

Pay

Salaries = annual rate

Perks = extras

Profits = linked to success

What does the specification require?

Human resource, are included in the specification mainly in the section on 'People in organisations'. You need to know about employment in businesses from the viewpoint of both the employee and the employer. You should therefore be aware of why people work, how they seek work and the rewards they expect from work, as well as how a business seeks workers, chooses the ones that it wants to employ and rewards them for their labour.

Different payment systems are covered under the sub-heading of 'Human needs and rewards'. They include wage rates such as time and piece rates, salaries, fringe benefits and non-financial rewards, along with incentive payments and systems such as bonuses and profit sharing. You should be able to advise a case study business of the most appropriate methods and explain why. You might also be asked to interpret and make calculations from pay slips.

Test yourself

Match each term with its correct definition:

1 contract rates		**a**	an additional benefit that comes with a job
2 perk		**b**	an annual amount usually paid in 12 monthly instalments
3 time rates		**c**	pay according to how much work has been done
4 profit sharing		**d**	pay linked to the number of hours worked
5 piece rates		**e**	pay linked to the profits of the business
6 overtime		**f**	pay made on the completion of a particular job
7 salary		**g**	the extra payment made for working outside usual hours

Try this

Question based on the 'Business and change' option

> Merrion's Garage Services Ltd is a private limited company owned by John Merrion and his family. Three of John's staff form the car wash and valet team. Recently, he has changed the way they are paid from time rate to piece rate.

Explain what this means and the effect it is likely to have on both the business and the employees. **(4 marks)**

Recruitment

Core knowledge

Recruitment is the process by which a business finds new staff. It is handled by human resources. This may be a separate department (perhaps called 'personnel') or may be just one of the jobs done by a manager or owner. In most cases, the process is the same. There are a number of reasons why a business might need to recruit new staff:

- The business might be growing.
- Staff could have left.
- The business may need new skills.

Retirement creates a need for recruitment

Internal or external?

The business has to decide whether to recruit from outside the business (external) or to train its own staff (internal). If it decides to recruit, the process is as follows:

- It identifies the job that needs doing.
- It writes a **job description** to show what tasks, skills and qualifications are needed.
- It writes a **person specification** to show the type of person it needs to recruit.
- It can then advertise vacancies. It is important that this is done in the right place.

The law

Businesses must conform to the law. Advertising (and the whole process of recruiting) must be fair and open; all groups must be treated equally. People who apply for a job are called 'applicants'. Applicants will say why they should have the job. They can do this in a letter of application or by providing a **CV** that shows they can do the job.

Selection

Human resources then goes through the selection process:

- It looks at applications and CVs and chooses the applicants it thinks are most likely to be good at the job. This is called the **short list**.
- Short-listed applicants are invited to interview. People coming to an interview are called 'candidates'.
- Interviews could be one-to-one, or in front of a panel. The interview might even involve tests to show that the candidate can really do the job.
- After the interviews, the preferred candidate is offered the job. If the candidate accepts, he or she is then appointed.

Expense

Recruiting can be very expensive. Sometimes no candidate is good enough for the job and the whole process has to be repeated. This is why businesses try to make sure they get it right first time.

Speak the language

CV — curriculum vitae — the job applicant's list of personal details, qualifications, education and experience

job description — this shows what tasks, skills and qualifications are needed

person specification — this shows the type of person the business needs to recruit

short list — the applicants most likely to be good at the job; these applicants will be interviewed

An interview panel

INGRAM

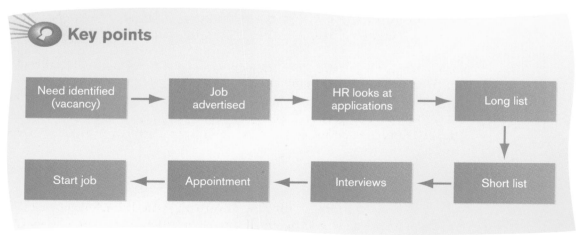

Key points

Need identified (vacancy) → Job advertised → HR looks at applications → Long list ↓

Start job ← Appointment ← Interviews ← Short list

What does the specification require?

Stages in recruitment and selection are included in the 'Management and recruitment' section of the specification. You need to know about the different ways of advertising for staff and the various stages of the recruitment process. This includes the documents used in recruitment and selection, such as the job description, person specification, advertisement, application form and CV. You must be able to relate these to the main stages in the recruitment process (e.g. identifying needs, advertising, receiving applications and selection).

Test yourself

Copy and complete the following sentences:

Human resources writes a .... to show what tasks, skills and qualifications are needed and a .... to show the sort of worker that will fit the requirements. It .... the post and invites .... Using letters and .... that are sent in, it draws up a .... of the .... it thinks are best qualified. These become .... and are invited to .... The successful .... is offered the job.

Try this

Core paper question

> Sarah is setting up a hairdressing business. She intends to employ one full-time member of staff to work during the week and two or three part-time staff to cover the weekend.

Sarah needs to draw up a person specification for the full-time post.

(a) What is meant by the term 'person specification'?   **(2 marks)**

(b) What details should Sarah include in this person specification? Explain why.   **(6 marks)**

Training, development and appraisal

Core knowledge

Training is the process of making sure that workers in a business have the knowledge and skills necessary to do the job. Training is seen as being of more benefit to the business than to the worker. It is needed to make sure that the business is operating as efficiently as possible. **Development** is different from training. It is seen as being of more benefit to the worker — developing his or her own skills and knowledge. Development may involve, for example, taking professional examinations or undertaking further study.

Training

Businesses have to decide whether to carry out training themselves, or use external agencies. Agencies can be more effective at training, but they tend to be expensive. Big businesses have their own training departments.

Training takes different forms depending on the stage that the worker is at — that is, whether he or she is a new appointee or one who has been with the business for some time.

Induction training

All new appointments to a business require some form of **induction training**. This is training to introduce staff to the workplace and the job. It includes basic training in processes and methods and also lets the new employee know what is usual in the business. This is called 'custom and practice' and covers issues such as when breaks or leave can be taken, and the basic operation of the workplace.

Further training

Further training may be either:

- on-the-job training, which happens at the place of work
- off-the-job training, using an external trainer, off site

Appraisal

Appraisal is the process used to see how well a worker is doing. It also allows the worker to exchange views with his or her employer. A good appraisal may result in rewards, or may be part of the path to promotion. Most businesses that have invested a lot of money and time in the training and development of employees will want to keep them and may operate a system of financial or other rewards (e.g. recognition and increased responsibility) in order to do so. Appraisal can help to identify where progress has been made.

Key points

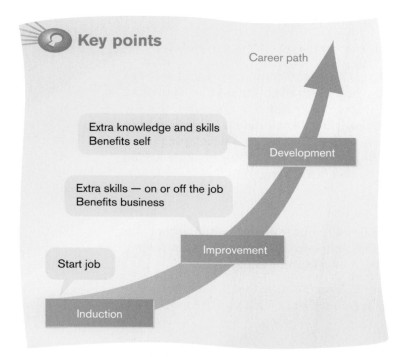

Boost your grade

Because of the difference between training and development, there can be a conflict of interest. A business may be keen to train a worker in its own methods and operations. This makes the worker more valuable to the business. On the other hand, the business may be reluctant to encourage development, as this makes the worker more flexible and more attractive to other businesses.

What does the specification require?

The specification looks at the reasons for training from the point of view of both the business and the individual's personal development. You need to know about different types of training, such as induction and specific skills training, as well as the main alternatives: internal/on-the-job and external/off-the-job training. You also need to show that you understand the importance of health and safety requirements and training, and how they affect business.

Test yourself

1 The process of developing the skills and knowledge that the business needs is called:

A recruitment   B training   C advertising

D interviewing   E development

2   The process of developing the skills and knowledge that the employee needs is called:

A recruitment   B training   C advertising
D interviewing   E development

3   The initial introduction to a business is usually called:

A initial training   B introduction training   C induction training
D initial development   E introductory development

4   The process of seeing how well a worker is doing and suggesting improvements is called:

A praise   B interviewing   C induction
D personal development   E appraisal

5   Training that takes place at the place of work is called:

A in the job   B at the job   C with the job
D on the job   E off the job

Try this

Core paper question

> Sarah is setting up a hairdressing business. She has employed one full-time member of staff to work during the week and three part-time staff.
>
> The part-time staff are starting this weekend. Sarah needs to draw up an induction training schedule for them.

(a) What is meant by 'induction training'?   **(2 marks)**
(b) Explain what areas need to be covered in such training.   **(6 marks)**

Rights and responsibilities at work

Core knowledge

Workers at a business have certain rights in law. They also have responsibilities. Workers have a right to decent working conditions and fair pay. In return, employers expect them to be punctual, efficient and loyal.

Health and safety

The main law regarding health and safety is the *Health and Safety at Work Act*, 1974. This law makes sure that all workers have proper washroom and toilet facilities, ventilation, fire exits and levels of heating and lighting.

Health and safety signs have to be clear

No unauthorised access

DANGER! Deep quarry

Basic employment rights

Basic employment rights include:

- safe, healthy and reasonably comfortable working conditions
- protection from danger in the workplace
- breaks and holidays

Most of these rights are laid down in employment law, although some are basic human rights, such as the right for an employee to be treated with courtesy and respect by an employer, and for the employee to treat the employer in the same way.

Rights in law

All employees have certain legal rights:

- They are entitled to a written statement giving rates of pay, terms and conditions of employment, pensions, notice periods, **disciplinary procedures** and so on. If a statement is not issued within 2 months of the employment starting, the employee can take the employer to an industrial tribunal, which will rule on what the conditions should be.
- They are entitled to join a trade union.
- They are entitled to the minimum wage.
- They have the right to an itemised pay statement.
- They have the right not to be unfairly dismissed and are entitled to a written statement of the reasons for their dismissal.
- They have the right to **redundancy** payments.
- Employees and employers have the right to a minimum **notice period** on either side.
- Workers also have the right, under EU laws, to take part in the management of the business for which they work.

Equality

The law states that in all matters of recruitment, selection, training, promotion and other areas of human resources, there should be no **discrimination** on grounds of gender, race, religion, creed, sexual orientation, disability or age. The main laws are as follows:

- *Equal Pay Act, 1970.* Men and women should receive equal pay for equal work. If a woman is doing the same work as a man, she should be paid the same wage.
- *Sex Discrimination Act, 1975.* This extended the law to take account of such things as recruitment and training and promotion opportunities.
- *Race Relations Act, 1976.* This made discrimination on the grounds of race or colour, marital status, nationality or ethnic group illegal and set up the Race Relations Board to investigate complaints.
- *Disability Discrimination Act, 1995.* Employers with 20 or more staff cannot discriminate against applicants or employees on grounds of disability, providing that they are capable of doing the job.
- *Age Discrimination Act, 2006.* This makes it unlawful to exclude people from jobs because of their age.

Speak the language

disciplinary procedure — the process that a worker has to go through if he or she has done something wrong at work

discrimination — acting against someone for a reason that is not connected to his or her ability to do the job, such as colour, gender or age

notice period — the amount of time an employee has to give before he or she leaves

redundancy — what happens to an employee when a job is no longer required, perhaps due to changes in technology

Boost your grade

Remember that the rights of workers have to be balanced against their responsibilities. For example, although it is the employer's job to make sure that the workplace is safe and healthy, the employee has a responsibility to take reasonable care and not act in a foolish manner.

What does the specification require?

Rights and responsibilities of labour are included in the 'Aiding and controlling business activity' section of the specification under 'Influences on business activity'. This topic covers the main features of contracts of employment, employment protection and equal opportunities legislation. You will never be asked to give specific examples of legislation or to date legislation, but you need a general understanding of why certain laws have been passed and what effect they have on a business.

 Key points

Rights relate to three areas:
- health and safety
- fairness — for example, in the matter of pay and terms and conditions of employment
- equality — equal treatment without discrimination

Test yourself

Without referring back, match each of the Acts listed below with its date:

1 Race Relations Act		**a**	1970
2 Equal Pay Act		**b**	1975
3 Disability Discrimination Act		**c**	1995
4 Sex Discrimination Act		**d**	2006
5 Age Discrimination Act		**e**	1976

Try this

Alternative paper to coursework question

Judith Smith works as a financial manager for Royaume and is based in Tinnerton. She has just found out that Rob Williams, who carries out the same job as her but is based in London, is paid almost twice as much as she is.

Judith is unhappy with this situation. Explain under what legislation she can seek compensation. What steps would you advise her to take?   **(4 marks)**

Industrial relations

Core knowledge

Industrial relations refers to the relationship between the employer/ employer's representatives and the employee/employee's representatives. Employer groups may be professional associations, employer associations or bodies representing particular industries. Employee groups are usually trade unions.

Collective bargaining

Employee groups and employer groups often negotiate on pay and conditions of work. Because these negotiations take place between representatives of groups, they are called **collective bargaining**.

Firefighters man a picket line as part of a 24-hour strike

Industrial action

An industrial dispute occurs when there is a breakdown of industrial relations. It can lead to industrial action being taken by one side or the other.

Employees

Employees can take various levels of industrial action. The main types are:

- **strikes**
- overtime bans
- working to rule (production is slowed down by all rules and regulations being followed to the letter)
- go-slows (continuing with the job but at a much reduced rate)

The most serious weapon is for employees to withdraw their labour altogether in a strike. Strikes may be selective, short (1-day strikes) or total. Striking workers may also **picket** to try to persuade others not to work. Strikes are damaging to both employers and employees.

Employers

On the employers' side, those in dispute may, in certain cases, be dismissed or the employer may refuse to allow them to work (a 'lock out').

Laws

Because such tactics are so damaging, there are laws to try to stop industrial disputes getting worse. Should negotiations break down, there are bodies in place to help. The main body is the Advisory, Conciliation and Arbitration Service (ACAS), which provides a service to help solve industrial disputes through negotiation and agreement. It can:

- advise
- conciliate – try to get the two sides to agree
- arbitrate – make a ruling between the two sides

Key points

- Industrial relations refers to the relationship between employers and employees.
- Industrial disputes occur when these relations break down.
- Industrial action is when one side or the other uses tactics to try to force agreement.

What does the specification require?

The study of industrial relations is included in the 'Aiding and controlling business activity' section of the specification, under 'Influences on business activity'. You need to be able to describe the work of trade unions, types of industrial action and the main methods of resolving conflict. For the 'Business and change' option, you should also be aware of how changes such as those in traditional working arrangements are managed, and about 'new' patterns of working such as teleworking and remote office working.

Test yourself

Define the difference between industrial relations, industrial disputes and industrial action.

Try this

Core paper question

> Fiveways Farm is a large dairy farm. It produces milk, cream and cheese, and has recently gone into making bio-yoghurts. Dan Farrer owns Fiveways. Dan has recently employed a manger, Asif, to help him run the business. Asif has discouraged staff from joining a union. He says that he would rather listen to individual workers than to union representatives. He claims that Fiveways's own policies are better and fairer than national policies agreed by unions and management in other parts of the industry.

Explain two possible advantages that trade unions could bring to Fiveways Farm employees.   **(6 marks)**

Motivation

Core knowledge

Motivation involves persuading people to do something because they want to — generally, because they can see a benefit from the action. In a business, motivated workers work harder or better either because they particularly want to please the boss, or because there is some form of reward to be had.

Sometimes a word of praise or congratulation is enough to motivate; sometimes it needs to be something more solid. In the case of a sole trader or other small business, the motivation may be to provide an income, or to show that they can be a success, or it could simply be to have independence.

Motivation theory

A number of writers have come up with theories of how to understand and motivate workers. If businesses can develop ways to motivate them, then they can become more efficient. The main theories are those of Abraham Maslow, Frederick Herzberg and Douglas McGregor.

Maslow

Maslow says that workers have a number of needs or wants, and are motivated towards achieving the higher ones. These range from basic survival needs to 'being happy' or 'fulfilled'. They are usually arranged in levels in a triangle (a **hierarchical pyramid**).

Herzberg

Herzberg found that motivation often came from a feeling of doing a job well, or being well thought of. He introduced the phrase, **hygiene factors**. These are conditions that he likened to good hygiene in a restaurant or similar setting. People expect it to be there and only notice if it is missing. In the same way, workers expect a reasonable wage and working conditions, so these are not motivating, but they are demotivating if they are missing. The key point of this theory is that decent pay is an expectation, rather than a motivating factor.

McGregor

McGregor proposed theories for two types of worker (and manager), which he called **Theory X** and **Theory Y**. X workers are basically work-shy and lazy, while Y workers are keen and want responsibility. Different approaches to motivation are therefore needed for the different groups.

In the real world

Businesses use a variety of ways to motivate workers, including bonuses, perks (e.g. prizes, healthcare and travel), and psychology (e.g. praise and promotion).

> ## Speak the language
>
> **hierarchical pyramid** — Maslow's illustration of the levels that people want to reach
>
> **hygiene factors** — Herzberg's conditions that people expect and only notice if they are missing
>
> **motivation** — this involves persuading people to do something because they want to
>
> **Theory X and Theory Y** — these refer to McGregor's two types of worker — one lazy, one keen

Maslow's hierarchy of needs

Self-actualisation: a complicated way of saying you've got to where you want to be

Status: knowing that people look up to you

Social: having friends and family

Security: being able to plan for the future

Survival needs: food, water, shelter

Boost your grade

Different people can be motivated in different ways, depending on their outlook and aims. If you are answering a question on motivation, you should not just list the theorists, but decide which theory is the most suitable for the situation given and, most importantly, give reasons why you think so. There are also many more modern theorists. You can quote these even if they are not listed on your specification.

Key points

The three main theorists and their theories are:

- Maslow — hierarchy of needs, try to get to the top
- Herzberg — hygiene factors — good pay and conditions are expected; more is needed to motivate
- McGregor — Theory X workers motivated by threats; Theory Y workers motivated by trust and responsibility

What does the specification require?

You need to know why both workers and businesses benefit from the use of methods of motivation. This includes the importance of the role of managers in motivating workers, and the ways in which such motivation may be achieved. In particular, you should be aware of how methods of motivation work because they fulfil human needs.

Test yourself

Copy this diagram and fill in the correct definitions of each level of Maslow's hierarchy.

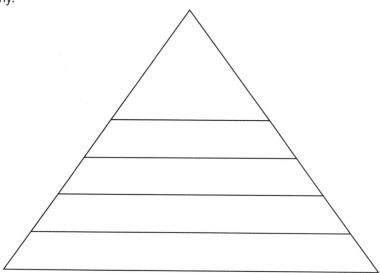

Try this

Core paper question

Sarah is setting up a hairdressing business. She has employed one full-time member of staff to work during the week and three part-time staff. Sarah needs to motivate her staff to work well.

Recommend one way to motivate the staff using money, and one way not using money. Explain your choices.   **(6 marks)**

Test on Chapter 5

Test your knowledge by writing as full an answer as possible to this question.

Extract from a case study

Royaume Ltd is a worldwide business, specialising in sports equipment, clothing and shoes. Its head office is in Tinnerton, a new town about 25 kilometres from London, but it has operations all around the globe, including other EU countries, North and South America, Asia and the Far East.

Royaume Ltd has a training programme for all its workers, to encourage them to develop new skills. Each worker is expected to improve his or her skills by attending at least one course a year. These include management training, foreign languages, ICT and sports coaching awards.

Analyse whether or not it is a good idea for employees to be required to undertake training in this way, from the point of view of both the employee and the business. Suggest whether such training is a good idea.   **(10 marks)**

Chapter 6
Production

Production is the key functional area for manufacturers and processors. It involves everything from finding the right location for a business to finding the right raw materials at the right prices, operating plant and equipment efficiently and maintaining quality systems.

Sub-departments of operations (or departments in their own right) are in charge of researching and developing new products and methods, finding more efficient ways to operate and deciding between alternative transport and distribution systems, as well as organising all transport of raw materials, parts, goods and partly finished goods.

The production area also has a key role to play in ensuring that the business turns out quality products, with as much efficiency and as little waste as possible.

Chain of production

Core knowledge

A good goes through several stages in its journey from raw materials to final consumer. The main stages of production are:
- obtaining raw materials
- processing, refining or manufacturing
- distribution and retailing

The raw materials have to be extracted or otherwise obtained, factories and plants are needed for manufacturing and processing, and various commercial functions (e.g. transport and insurance) are necessary before the good reaches the final consumer. Sometimes production requires a lot of labour (labour intensive) and sometimes machinery is used (capital intensive). The balance between labour and capital is just one of the many production decisions.

INGRAM

Chain of production

The chain of production describes the path of a product from raw material to final consumer. Most products pass through three distinct stages and industry can be put into categories that reflect these stages.

Primary industry

The first stage of the process is called **primary production**. This involves extracting raw materials. It includes any industry that takes a material in its natural state and turns it into a resource that can be used in the production process. Examples include fishing, farming and forestry, along with the more obvious mining, quarrying and drilling for oil.

Secondary industry

The second stage of the process is called **secondary production**. Secondary industry involves taking the raw materials and turning them into finished or part-finished goods. It therefore includes processes such as refining, processing and manufacture.

Drilling for oil is an example of primary production

Tertiary industry

The third stage of the process is called **tertiary production**. Tertiary industry is not just the final stage in a product's life — from manufacturer to wholesaler, retailer and consumer — but also includes all the other services that are provided to support primary and secondary industry. Insurance, banking, communications and other support services are all part of the tertiary sector (along with direct services such as transport and retailing).

The complete chain of production also includes:
- wholesalers: these buy in bulk, sell in smaller units (called 'breaking bulk') and provide storage
- retailers: these include all points where a consumer can buy the good, ranging from traditional shops to vending machines, and from catalogues to online retailers

Transformation

Transformation is what is happening in the chain — one material is being transformed into another. Raw materials are made into finished goods, components put together, and manufactured goods delivered to wholesalers and retailers.

Speak the language

primary production — the first stage of the production process, dealing with raw materials

secondary production — the second stage of production, dealing with making the good

tertiary production — the third stage of production, dealing with services

Manufacturers are involved in secondary production

Categories of countries

The stage of development that a country has reached is sometimes stated in terms of its main types of industry. The UK is considered to be a developed economy. It has a very large service sector, a shrinking manufacturing (secondary) sector and a relatively small primary sector. Countries such as Brazil, India and Malaysia are rapidly developing a manufacturing base. Other countries — including many African ones — rely on raw material production.

Key points

Traditional long-chain distribution; stages can be cut out to shorten it

Boost your grade

Remember that at each stage of the chain a good becomes more valuable as 'value is added'. This is because a process or service has been undertaken. The further down the chain, the more processes or services have been used, so the nearer the good will be to its final price.

What does the specification require?

Production is included in the specification in a number of areas. 'Business activity' covers how production adds value and the classification of industry, but also looks at how customer needs are met in a competitive environment. Under 'Business behaviour', production covers the organisation of resources, methods of production, economies and diseconomies of scale, costs and quality issues. You need to be able to show your understanding by giving examples from case study businesses — for instance, of appropriate production methods.

The 'Business and change' option covers the location of industry.

Regarding the content of this section, you need to know how an economy is classified into local or national businesses, those that can be assigned to

primary, secondary and tertiary sectors, and how they work together. The specification places some emphasis on how the sectors have changed — in particular, the decline of the primary and manufacturing sectors and the growth of the tertiary sector in the UK. Questions on the distribution aspects of production are more likely to be found in the context of the marketing mix.

Test yourself

1 Draw a diagram showing the stages of production, from raw material extration to consumer. Label and define each stage.

2 Draw a diagram showing traditional long-chain distribution. Label and define each stage.

Try this

Question based on the 'Business and change' option

> Merrion's Garage Services Ltd is a private limited company owned by John Merrion and his family. Merrion's is part of the tertiary sector of the economy.

(a) Explain the term 'tertiary sector' and give another example of a business in this sector. **(2 marks)**

(b) John Merrion says that tertiary sector businesses must 'stay close to their customers'. Explain how businesses can achieve this. **(4 marks)**

Methods of production

Core knowledge

Production or 'transformation' is the process by which raw materials and other inputs, such as components, are turned into outputs, and eventually into the final product. The method of production depends on the nature of the product and the nature of the customer. Services are almost always produced to individual standards for individual customers — for example, you can only wear your own haircut. In the case of goods, some will be produced for a mass market, where the fact that they are all identical may be of benefit. The main methods of production are job, batch and flow. The scale of production refers to the size of a production run, which ranges from mass production to one-off production.

Hairdressing is an example of job production, as every customer has individual requirements

The same model of car produced in different colours is an example of batch production

Job production

Job production involves making a 'one-off' product to individual specifications — for example, made-to-measure clothes, a fitted kitchen or a customised car. This tends to be the most labour-intensive production method, and can lead to expensive outputs due to the craft skills that are usually needed.

Batch production

In **batch production** the same machinery and labour can be used to produce different batches or groups of products. Batch production takes place in any manufacturing process where different sizes or colours are needed. For example, the same dress may be produced in sizes from 8 to 16.

Flow production

Flow production is also called mass, continuous or process production. This involves a product being assembled or built as it moves along a production line. Examples are car manufacture (production line) and oil refining (processing). Flow production allows modern businesses to use automation. This means making certain processes automatic; some are even carried out by robots.

Economies and diseconomies of scale

Businesses can gain benefits from large-scale production. These are either internal (within the control of the business) or external (outside its control). Internal economies are:

- technical — bigger machines and more automated production are possible
- managerial — e.g. specialist managers can be employed
- trading — e.g. resources can be bought in bulk
- financial — e.g. bigger businesses can borrow more, and more easily

External economies include those gained from location, such as the availability of a skilled labour force or the reputation of an area. There can also be diseconomies, such as poor communication, slow decision making and employees feeling distanced from the business.

Speak the language

batch production — using the same machinery to make slightly different products

economies/diseconomies of scale — the advantage/ disadvantage of large-scale production

flow production — mass production on a production line

job production — making 'one-offs' to order

just-in-time — method when parts etc. arrive just as they are needed

lean production — cutting down on the use of workers, machinery and time

Lean production

Lean production involves being more efficient by minimising the use of all the inputs necessary for production, especially time. The main version of lean production is the **just-in-time** (JIT) approach. This means that parts, components and other materials arrive just as they are needed. There is therefore no need for stock to be held, or for a business to have the costs of storage. Of course, this means an efficient distribution system is essential – if stock or parts do not arrive 'just in time', the whole process is stopped.

Kanban is a Japanese system of stock control which gives workers responsibility for stock flows and is designed to ensure a continuous supply of stock.

 **Key points**

Production method	Numbers	Machinery	Example
Job	'One-offs'	Special tools	Haircut, wedding dress
Batch	Groups of similar products	Can be used to produce slightly different batches	Anything in different colours, sizes or varieties (e.g. clothes)
Flow	Mass production production line	Computers, robots, (e.g. freezers, televisions)	Cars, consumer goods

Boost your grade

When looking at questions of production, think about the inputs (e.g. raw materials, labour, machinery) that will be needed, the product itself (does it need to be uniform or made-to-measure?) and the intended market. This will lead you to the correct (or at least the most efficient) production method. Note that sometimes methods are combined – mass production may involve producing cars in batches, for example.

What does the specification require?

The main methods of production tested are job, batch and flow, but you should also be aware that in modern industry different types of production are often combined for greater efficiency. You should know about 'new' ideas such as lean production, and Japanese techniques such as kaizen, kanban and just-in-time. You need to be able to recommend different types of production according to the business circumstance provided. The development of automated production and its effect on the labour force may be studied under the 'Business and change' option. You must be clear about the advantages and disadvantages that might arise due to the scale of production. For higher-order marks, you should be able to link the costs of production with financial tools such as breakeven analysis.

Test yourself

1 The production method when parts etc. arrive only as they are needed is called:

A test-in-time   B not-in-time   C just-in-time
D batch production   E mean production

2 Production that cuts down on the use of workers, machinery and time is called:

A job production   B flow production   C batch production
D lean production   E clean production

3 Producing large quantities on a production line is called:

A job production   B flow production   C batch production
D lean production   E clean production

4 Using the same machinery and inputs to make slightly different products is called:

A job production   B flow production   C batch production
D lean production   E clean production

5 Making one-off products to order is called:

A job production   B flow production   C batch production
D lean production   E clean production

Try this

Core paper question

Fiveways Farm Ltd is a large dairy farm. It produces milk, cream and cheese, and has recently gone into making bio-yoghurts. Dan Farrer owns Fiveways and is in charge of all the production. His wife, Janet, is in charge of marketing and sales, while their son, Jeb, is in charge of all the finances and accounts.

Explain the possible benefits and drawbacks of this division of labour.

(6 marks)

Management of quality

Core knowledge

A **quality** good or service is one that does what it is supposed to do. It is one that is, in UK law, 'fit for purpose'. If the product does not do what it should, the consumer has the right to demand his or her money back. It is therefore vital that businesses make products that are reliable and that consumers will continue to buy. A business usually sets up its own quality systems to make sure that production standards are even better than the consumer expects. Businesses look at what the law requires and then add to this in order to please the consumer and beat their competitors.

A quality watch doesn't have to be gold — it just needs to tell the time

Quality control systems

Traditional **quality control** systems check that the finished product has reached the required standard. The problem with this system is that the product has already been made, and must therefore be wasted if it is not up to scratch. This is particularly true where a process is involved (e.g. baking and food manufacture, refining and painting) and ingredients or other inputs cannot be recovered. In some industries, at least some materials can be recovered: paper, for instance, can be re-pulped. In other cases, products are written off.

Statistical process control

Statistical process control is part of a quality control system. Inputs, outputs and machinery are all checked at regular intervals (decided by statistics). This means that any slight adjustment that needs to be made to a machine, or to the way a product is being made, should be detected very early on and put right. This system is not enough, however, to ensure that no poor-quality products are made.

TQM

TQM stands for **total quality management**. This is a system that was first developed in Japan. The idea is that every single person involved in production is responsible for quality. Each worker (and each machine) checks for quality as the product enters their area, as it is processed, and before it leaves. The process

Speak the language

ISO 9001 — an international standard of quality

kaizen — the Japanese idea of continuous improvement

quality — describes a good or service that does what it is supposed to do

quality control — systems that check that the finished product has reached the required standard

statistical process control — part of a quality control system where checks are made at statistically defined intervals

total quality management (TQM) — all workers are responsible for quality at all stages

extends to parts, materials and other inputs. A truly TQM business only deals with other TQM businesses.

Kaizen

Another Japanese idea linked to quality is **kaizen**. This means 'continuous improvement' and states that it is every worker's job to see how their process could be made more efficient (however small that change). In this way, many small changes lead to improvements in quality and efficiency. Efficient production is vital to profitability, so businesses are keen to measure efficiency. Measures include productivity (number produced per time period or set of inputs), unit cost (cost to produce one product) and percentage use of resources (e.g. is a particular machine used 90 % or 100% of the time?).

ISO 9001

There are international standards of quality that businesses can earn. These show other businesses (and customers) that this business is keen to maintain quality. One of the most important is **ISO 9001**. This is an international standard that has to be renewed every year to show that the business is still maintaining quality. The kite mark, in the UK, is also used to show that products have passed quality tests set by the British Standards Institute (BSI).

Key points

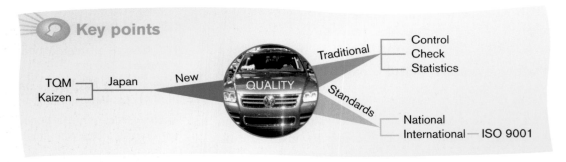

What does the specification require?

You need to know about the importance of quality in general, and about quality assurance and other techniques used to ensure quality production. Specifically, you need to be able to explain what is meant by quality assurance, the methods by which it can be achieved, and why it is important to businesses in a competitive environment.

You might be asked to think about the key decisions that face the case study business in planning how to maintain quality. You might need to discuss the advantages and disadvantages of various methods and, for higher-order marks, be asked to recommend a particular method to the business example provided.

Test yourself

Read the key terms and their definitions on page 109 and then, without looking at them, write a definition of:

➤ quality
➤ quality control
➤ statistical process control
➤ TQM
➤ kaizen
➤ ISO 9001

Try this

Alternative paper to coursework question

Royaume shoes are produced by Schwitt plc, a subsidiary of the company. The shoes are sold in a very competitive market. John Young is one of the directors of Schwitt plc, and explains that 'to maintain our quality, we have introduced a TQM system, rather than the old-style quality checks'.

Suggest and explain how a TQM system (total quality management) could be better than quality checks. **(6 marks)**

Business location

Core knowledge

Businesses need to decide not only what they are going to sell, but also where they are going to sell from. All businesses, even online ones, need somewhere to trade from. The ideal location will not be too expensive, but will help the business to attract customers. Businesses therefore look at costs as one factor, but may have to deal with several other factors, including customers, services and supplies. For some businesses, a single factor will stand out; for others, a combination of factors will be important.

Natural factors

Some businesses can only be located near natural factors that are essential to them. The most obvious of

Location may not be a matter of choice

ROBERTO BURGOS S. COSTA RICA

Speak the language

bulk decreasing — when a product loses weight or volume during production/processing

bulk increasing — when a product gains weight or volume during production/processing

infrastructure — roads, railways, airports, power, communications etc.

these are those businesses dealing in extracting raw materials — they can only operate where the raw materials may be found. For other businesses, there could be other requirements — for example:

- a source of water for washing textiles
- hazardous operations, such as nuclear power generation, being kept away from residential areas
- a particular climate for growing a crop

Some of these factors may be important for historical reasons that are no longer relevant, but businesses tend to find it more expensive to move than to stay where they are already established.

Bulk increasing and decreasing

The production process takes goods from raw materials to finished product. Sometimes this involves a decrease in volume, sometimes an increase. In the case of furniture, for example, it is easier to transport the raw material (wood) than the finished item — this is a **bulk-increasing** industry. In the case of orange juice, it is easier to transport the boxed or bottled finished product than the actual oranges because it is **bulk decreasing**. The business should locate where transport costs will be lowest.

Customers

Customers need to be able to buy from the business. To do this, they may need to visit a shop or other retail outlet. This means that such outlets need display and storage space along with parking facilities or public transport for customers. One

Dell only sells online

way around this is to allow customers to view stock and buy online. Some businesses have done away with retail outlets altogether.

Suppliers

Suppliers need to be able to access the business in order to deliver goods and services. Although a business in a remote location may have lower rents, suppliers may be reluctant to visit. Businesses may therefore find that they rely on a good **infrastructure** in order to be able to keep both customers and suppliers happy.

Workers

In some cases, a business may need a large workforce, or a workforce with particular qualifications or specialisms. Some areas of the country are known for certain skills, so similar businesses have been attracted there in the past. The 'potteries' around Stoke-on-Trent are one example.

Government

There are government grants and other packages of assistance to help businesses set up in certain areas. Usually, this is where a traditional business has gone into decline. Many areas that have declining industry and high unemployment have been labelled 'assisted areas' and are helped in this way. The European Union also provides regional assistance.

Boost your grade

Always try to include examples to illustrate your answers about location. Think about the businesses near where you live or study. What sort of reasons do they have for being there? Although some reasons may be historical, why have they decided to remain there?

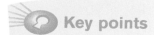 **Key points**

Location factors include:

- natural or geographical factors
- the nature of the product or process
- location and ease of access for customers
- location and ease of access for suppliers
- location and skills of workers
- national and international government assistance

What does the specification require?

The specification includes location in its 'Business and change' option. You should be aware of the pull of the market and customers, as against the pull of production, and be able to identify other key factors that influence the location of business and industry. You should be able to make decisions about location and pass this advice to the business given in the scenario.

Test yourself

Copy and complete the following sentences:

The production process takes goods from .... to .... Sometimes this involves a decrease in volume, sometimes an increase. A .... industry is one where the product becomes harder to transport as it passes through the process. An example is .... being turned into .... A .... industry is one where the product becomes easier to transport as it passes through the process. An example is .... being turned into .... The business should locate where .... will be lowest.

Try this

Question based on the 'Business communication and marketing' option

PetsFirst sells a range of specialist pet foods and pet accessories via a mail order catalogue. The company plans to open an e-commerce centre to cope with its web-based sales. This is over 300 kilometres away from its current base. The company is going to locate it in an Enterprise Zone, where special assistance is available from the government.

(a) Explain the term 'e-commerce'. **(2 marks)**
(b) Explain the possible benefits and problems of locating in an Enterprise Zone. **(6 marks)**

Test on Chapter 6

Test your knowledge by writing as full an answer as possible to this question.

Extract from a case study

Merrion's Garage Services Ltd is a private limited company owned by John Merrion and his family. Merrion's is part of the tertiary sector of the economy.

The business sells cars and accessories. It also services and valets vehicles. John Merrion is considering limiting the suppliers to his business to those businesses that are able to guarantee quality.

(a) Suggest why this is a good idea. **(3 marks)**
(b) Explain three ways in which Merrion's could guarantee quality of supply. **(6 marks)**

Chapter 7
Marketing

Marketing involves finding out what the customer (or possible future customer) wants and then producing a good or service at a price that he or she will be willing to pay. Market research is the area that tries to find out what is wanted; it is then up to research and development and production to make the product. Products can be market-orientated (designed to please a particular market) or product-oriented (designed and then the market persuaded to buy it).

Four key areas come together in marketing the product. These are the four parts of the 'marketing mix': price, product, promotion and place. They are often just known as the 'four Ps', but this is slightly misleading as 'place' is really distribution. Some people think that a fifth 'P' for 'packaging' should also be included.

In examinations it is important to remember and point out that each of these areas is just one part of the marketing mix, and that it is vital to get the balance right. It is no use having a fantastic product if no one knows about it, or if it can only be made at a price that no one is willing to pay. Equally, there is no point in promoting something that is not available or that cannot be transported to where customers want to buy it.

Market research

Core knowledge

Businesses need to collect **information** to help them sell products to their customers. They need to know:

■ who might buy the product

Market research

- what they might be willing to spend
- how often they might buy
- why they want to buy

They can find out this information through various means, such as asking questions or looking at market **data**. With this information the business can decide not only what to sell, but also how to change a product or develop new ones. Customers are divided into different groups so that they can be targeted more effectively. This is called market segmentation. Markets are divided (or segmented) by factors such as age, gender, income and hobbies. Key groups linked to income, education and employment are called 'socio-economic' groups.

Businesses can also use tools such as SWOT analysis. This looks at the internal Strengths and Weaknesses of a business and the external Opportunities and Threats. Internal factors can be changed by the business, external ones are outside its control. Businesses may collect the data themselves or use a specialist agency.

The most common way of dividing research is into **field research** and **desk research**.

Field research

Field research is also called primary research. It means that data are being collected for the first time. Field research is often carried out using:

- questionnaires — lists of questions asked of a **target audience**
- surveys — collecting information — for example, on buying habits; till roll information is often used
- observations — watching how customers behave
- focus groups — small groups of people are asked for their opinions and encouraged to discuss products
- tasting and testing — collecting feedback from people allowed to try the product

Field research is more accurate if the right people (sample) are asked. A random sample just asks anyone. A targeted sample uses a particular group (boys or girls, say). A quota sample makes sure that the group sampled reflects the make-up of a larger group — for example, if half of the population are male, a quota sample would be 50% male.

Desk research

Desk research is also called secondary research. It uses data and information that have already been collected.

The main sources for desk research are:

■ books
■ newspapers and journals
■ reports — company reports are free, but many market reports are expensive
■ the internet

Advantages and disadvantages

Field research:

■ makes sure that the data collected are exactly what is needed
■ is up to date
■ is expensive
■ can be time consuming

Desk research:

■ can be cheap or even free
■ can be expensive when obtaining particular information
■ is not necessarily exactly what is wanted
■ can be out of date
■ can be very unreliable

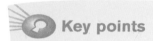 **Key points**

	Field research	**Desk research**
Advantages	Up to date Targeted	Cheap, even free Easy to obtain
Disadvantages	Expensive Time consuming Large surveys needed for accuracy	Out of date Not exactly what is wanted Some can be expensive

Boost your grade

Make sure that you know the difference between data and information. This can be really useful when answering case-study style questions where data have been provided. Ask yourself: how valid are the data (look at their source) and have they already been interpreted? Interpreted data are less reliable than any raw data with which you have been provided.

What does the specification require?

Marketing is covered in 'Business behaviour' and in the 'Business communication and marketing' option. You need to know about the various stages of marketing from initial market research through to the use of the marketing mix to persuade customers to buy. For the option, you need to be able to describe the importance of marketing to the survival and growth of a firm in a changing business environment. You should also understand how SWOT analysis can be used as a marketing tool and the simple application of supply and demand to marketing.

You need to know how a business finds out about markets and potential markets using both primary and secondary research. You may be asked to show how research has been carried out, recommend how it could be carried out, or comment or advise on research results. You should understand about market segmentation and be able to show how a market could be segmented — for example, through the use of socioeconomic groups. You need to understand that there are a number of different ways in which market research can be carried out, and may be asked to give an opinion on which is the most suitable for given situations.

For the 'Business communication and marketing' option, you should be able to distinguish between different types of market, such as niche and mass, and understand what is meant by test marketing. You should also be clear on the different models of data sampling, such as random and quota sampling.

Test yourself

Without looking at the key points, list the advantages and disadvantages of field research and desk research.

Try this

Question based on the 'Business communication and marketing' option

PetsFirst sells a range of specialist pet foods and pet accessories via a mail order catalogue. A major food company has just announced that it is to start selling a range of specialist cat and dog food. PetsFirst currently only sells goods in the UK. It has carried out a SWOT analysis to determine the strength of its market position. The result is shown here.

S	**W**
● Good product range ● Quality products ● Existing customers ● Cater to specialist market	● Specialist market is small ● Market is narrow
O	**T**
● Overseas expansion ● Internet sales ● New markets ● New products	● New competition

(a) Explain what is meant by the term 'SWOT analysis'. **(2 marks)**

(b) Explain two actions the owners could take as a result of the analysis. **(4 marks)**

Product

Core knowledge

The **product** is the good or service that is produced as a result of business activity. Without a product the business has nothing to sell. Goods can be touched and felt; services are 'invisible'. Some businesses sell a variety of products (**product range**); others sell just one.

Goods

There are three main types of good:
- *Consumer durables* can be used again and again ('durable' means 'lasting'), even though they will eventually wear out. They range from toothbrushes to cars.
- *Consumer non-durables* can only be used once; examples are petrol and toothpaste.
- *Industrial goods* are used as part of the production process and include factories, plants, equipment and tools.

Services

There are two main types of service:
- *Personal services* are for individuals and groups, such as plumbing, entertainment, taxi rides and tourism.
- *Commercial services* include insurance, retailing and transport.

Entertainment is a type of service

Product range

Product range refers to the different product lines that a business sells, such as a range of snack foods. The product mix refers to the variety of product types. A narrow mix means that the business is dependent on a particular market segment and therefore vulnerable to changes.

Product differentiation

Product differentiation involves businesses trying to make their products different from those of their competitors. One of the major ways of achieving this is through **branding**. Establishing a brand image may mean establishing a name, logo and other marks. These range

Speak the language

branding — creating an image for a product or range of products

product — the good or service that a business is selling

product differentiation — where businesses try to make their products different from those of their competitors

product range — the variety of products that a business sells

from the use of a particular style of lettering (e.g. Coca-Cola) through the use of particular colours (e.g. Ferrari's red) to the use of signs or signals (e.g. the three stripes of Adidas).

Boost your grade

Remember the importance of branding. It can persuade consumers to buy, even though the product may not be any good. Products are usually bought for 'core' (central) reasons and 'peripheral' (on the edge) reasons. The core reason for buying a top may be to stay warm; the peripheral reason may be the brand. A successful brand can become the main reason for buying.

Key points

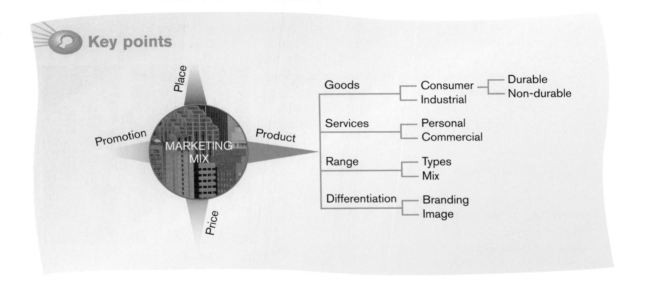

What does the specification require?

You should examine the product as part of the marketing mix, including ideas such as product design and packaging. You might also be asked to show why a business has a product range, and how brand names are used in marketing. You need to understand that the product can be a good or service, and might need to explain what is meant by a quality product. It is important that you understand that the product is just one part of the marketing mix, and that it is the balance of price, product, promotion and distribution that is important. In the 'Marketing and the business environment' option, you might need to demonstrate a basic understanding of the way in which demand and supply analysis is used in a marketing context.

Test yourself

1 A product aimed at businesses is called:

A a consumer durable   B a consumer non-durable
C an industrial service   D a personal service
E a commercial service

2 A product that lasts, and can be used many times, is called:

A a consumer durable good   B a consumer non-durable good
C an industrial good   D a personal service
E a commercial service

3 A good that can only be used once is called:

A a consumer durable good   B a consumer non-durable good
C an industrial good   D a personal service
E a commercial service

4 A product aimed at a consumer, for his or her own use, is usually called:

A a consumer durable good   B a consumer non-durable good
C an industrial good   D a personal service
E a commercial service

5 A product used by businesses to make other products is usually called:

A a consumer durable good   B a consumer non durable good
C an industrial good   D a personal service
E a commercial service

Try this

Core paper question

> Fiveways Farm Ltd is a large dairy farm. It produces milk, cream and cheese, and has recently gone into making bio-yoghurts. Dan Farrer owns Fiveways. Dan thinks that his venture into yoghurts has been a success and is now thinking of other lines that he might be able to sell. This is called product diversification.

Explain what is meant by 'product diversification' and why Dan is considering this. Give examples of possible options for Fiveways Farm.   **(6 marks)**

Product life cycles

Core knowledge

The **product life cycle** shows the usual stages through which a product passes. All products have a life cycle. Some are very short, or explosive. Others are very long or extended. The stage of the life cycle a product is at is important to a business. It shows it what sort of promotion or other changes might be needed to boost sales.

Normal life cycle

The typical product life cycle is shown opposite. Each stage can vary in length of time. The overall length of the product life cycle also differs from product to product. A really long product life cycle is that for KitKat bars — they have been going for over 60 years. A really short life cycle is that for World Cup flags. This lasted just a few months. Both, however, follow the same pattern.

The product life cycle

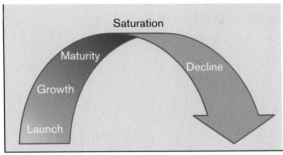

Stages

- *Development.* This can be a very long period for some products when costs are high. No sales are being made, so there is no revenue.
- *Launch.* This is when the product is first offered for sale and revenue starts to come in. Costs can still be high, as the product needs to be advertised.
- *Growth.* Sales grow as the product becomes better known; competitors will take note of a successful product and begin to think about bringing out rival ones.
- *Maturity.* By this stage, many people have bought the product; a brand is established but there are also now competitors; promotion is still needed.
- *Saturation.* The market is 'full' — every-one who is going to buy the product has done so and there are many competitor products.

Speak the language

cosmetic changes — changes that are not 'real', such as changes to packaging or lettering rather than to the product

extension strategies — extra value added or extra promotion designed to boost sales

product life cycle — the usual stages through which a product passes from development to withdrawal

■ *Decline*. At this point, as sales fall, the business must decide whether to try to extend the life cycle or let the product die.

Extension strategies

Successful products can have their life cycle extended through product **extension strategies**. These may involve:
■ changes to the product (real or **cosmetic changes**)
■ finding new uses or applications for the product
■ additional promotion
■ additions to the product range (e.g. Persil automatic, Persil colour, Persil biological)

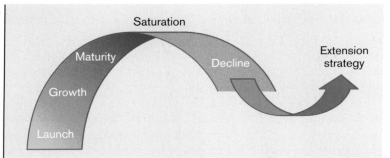

The extended product life cycle

Other life cycles

The following additional types of product life cycle have been identified:
■ Extended life cycles are where product extension is a success.
■ Aborted life cycles are where a product fails to find a market.
■ Explosive life cycles are where a product goes through the stages of the cycle very quickly — a Christmas craze, for instance.

The explosive life cycle

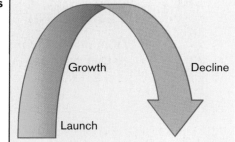

Boost your grade

Show your overall knowledge by linking life cycle to promotion. One of the most important features of the product life cycle is that managers can use it to change and develop promotion strategies. Whether or not it is worth spending money to promote a product may well depend on its position in its life cycle.

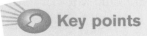

Key points

Stage	Description
1 Launch	The product is first brought out and introduced to the shops.
2 Growth	Sales grow as the product is advertised and becomes well known.
3 Maturity	Sales slow down. Most people have one, and now there are competing products.
4 Saturation	Sales start to go down. Everybody's got one already. There are many competing products, which are often cheaper and better.
5 Decline	Sales fall further. The product is eventually withdrawn from the market.

What does the specification require?

The use of product life cycle is most likely to be linked to how it is used as a tool by a business in relation to its marketing strategy — how different strategies are appropriate at different stages of the cycle. For example, you might be asked to recommend what sort of promotion should be considered for a product at a particular stage of its life cycle.

Test yourself

Copy the following diagram and label it with the correct terms. Provide a definition for each stage.

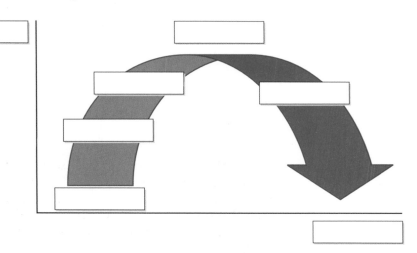

Try this

Question based on the 'Business communication and marketing' option

PetsFirst sells a range of specialist pet foods and pet accessories via a mail order catalogue.

The range of goods sold includes specialist food for dogs, cats and caged birds; toys for dogs and cats; cage toys for budgies; collars and novelties with pet pictures, such as calendars, tea towels and place mats.

PetsFirst is considering extending its product range to sell bird cages and is looking at the data shown in these two graphs (the year is 2010).

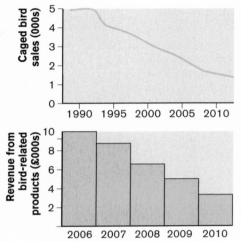

Suggest reasons why PetsFirst should not go ahead with offering bird cages.

(6 marks)

Price

Core knowledge

Price multiplied by the number of sales equals **revenue**. A business would like its revenue at least to cover costs (**breakeven**). The price of a product may be linked to a number of different factors including:

- the costs of production
- the price of competing products
- the amount of profit required
- the need for faster sales
- the stage the product is at in its life cycle

Cost-plus pricing

The most common form of pricing is probably **cost-plus pricing**. The business adds up the various costs of producing the product and then adds on a percentage for profit (called a **mark-up**). If a good cost £1 and there was a 25% mark-up, the price would be £1.25. The mark-up is linked to what a business feels a consumer will pay. A designer good, for instance, will have a very high mark-up.

A £5,000 dress: how much is cost, how much is mark-up?

TOPFOTO

Competitive pricing

Most other methods of pricing can be called competitive, as they involve pricing in such a way that the business sells more products than a competitor. Typical pricing strategies are:

- skimming — a product (often new technology) is sold at a high opening price to those who want to be first to own it
- penetration pricing — a product is sold at an initial low price to gain market share
- predatory pricing (destroyer pricing) — a business deliberately undercuts rivals in an attempt to remove them from the market

Some competitive pricing merely involves looking at what rivals are charging and matching this price.

Promotional pricing

Some pricing strategies are about promoting sales in the short term. Examples are:

- loss leaders — where a product is priced so low that it does not even cover its costs. This may be to attract buyers, who will then realise the benefits of the product and continue to buy it. In retail terms, the good is usually a staple product (such as bread or milk) priced to attract customers into the shop so that they spend money on other products.
- psychological point pricing — where prices are deliberately set below certain 'trigger' prices such as £5 or £100. Products seem cheaper when they are £4.99 or £99.99.

Key points

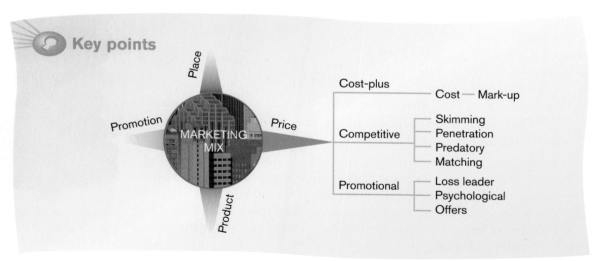

What does the specification require?

There are many different ways for a business to set the price of its products. You need to know about the most common of these. Perhaps most important is cost-plus pricing, as this is intended to make the business profitable. It is important to understand that price is just one part of the marketing mix, and that it is the balance of price, product, promotion and distribution that is important.

Test yourself

Match each term with its correct definition.

1 predatory pricing	**a** where a product is sold at a high opening price to those who want to be first to own it
2 psychological point pricing	**b** where a product can be sold at an initial low price to gain market share
3 loss leaders	**c** where a business deliberately undercuts rivals in an attempt to remove them from the market
4 skimming	**d** looking at what rivals are charging and matching this price
5 price matching	**e** where a product is priced below cost to attract buyers so that they spend money on other products
6 penetration pricing	**f** where prices are deliberately set below certain 'trigger' prices

Try this

Core paper question

Sarah is setting up a hairdressing business. She has looked at the competitors to her business in the local area and has to make a decision about what sort of prices to charge.

Should Sarah charge lower or higher prices than her competitors? Explain the reasons for your decision. **(8 marks)**

Promotion

Core knowledge

Promotion refers to the methods that businesses use to communicate to consumers, first, that their product exists and, second, that it has features that a consumer will like. Promotion is therefore used to inform consumers and to try to persuade them to buy. Products such as industrial goods may be promoted in different ways through, for example, trained salespeople who describe product benefits directly or through trade fairs and exhibitions.

Industrial goods are promoted through trade fairs

TOPFOTO

Speak the language

advertising agencies — specialist businesses that bid for advertising 'accounts' and plan the campaigns for other businesses

loyalty cards — these allow consumers to collect 'points' or similar, which can be exchanged for 'gifts'; the more each consumer buys, the more points he/she gains

point-of-sale material — placards, posters and display materials that are used at the point where the customer pays

Campaigns

Promotion is often carried out through campaigns. These are a mixture of different types of promotion. A typical promotional campaign may include television advertising, poster campaigns, new labelling, competitions and special offers. Smaller businesses are helped by campaigns aimed at the products they are selling. Larger businesses may launch their own campaigns. Often businesses use specialist **advertising agencies**.

Above-the-line

Advertising is publicity for a product that is paid for directly; it is therefore called 'above-the-line' expenditure. Advertising is used to promote products through broadcast and print media such as television, radio, posters, magazines, leaflets and **point-of-sale material**.

In the UK, advertising is regulated by the Advertising Standards Authority. This makes sure that all advertisements are legal, decent and honest.

Below-the-line

Below-the-line expenditure is promotion other than direct advertising. It is not paid for directly. In promoting a product to a consumer, a business may use various techniques, such as money-off coupons, special offers, competitions, free samples and trials, and **loyalty cards**.

Packaging

Packaging is used to protect goods, but can also be used to promote products. Goods can be packed in particular colours or styles to attract customers. Even services can be 'packaged' — a customer ordering a kitchen, for instance, may want a 'package' of design, fitting, tiling and finishing as well as the goods.

PR

Public relations (PR) is a term that can be used to cover any way of generating publicity. PR is designed to build a particular image in the mind of the consumer. Methods include sponsorship, endorsement and product placement.

- Sponsorship means that the product will be associated with a certain event or sport, or what is good about the event — a marathon would promote fitness, for instance.
- Endorsement is when a celebrity is persuaded to say or show that he or she thinks a particular product is worth having. Businesses may give products to celebrities in the hope of gaining free publicity of this kind.
- Product placement involves giving products for use in films or television shows, in the hope that the product will be seen on screen.

Formula 1 racing is heavily sponsored

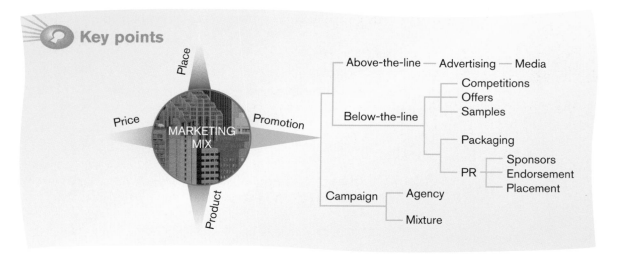

Key points

- Marketing Mix: Place, Price, Product, Promotion
  - Above-the-line — Advertising — Media
  - Below-the-line
    - Competitions
    - Offers
    - Samples
    - Packaging
    - PR
      - Sponsors
      - Endorsement
      - Placement
  - Campaign
    - Agency
    - Mixture

Boost your grade

You should be able to argue for and against advertising. The main case in favour of advertising is that it informs — without it, customers would not know what was on offer and would therefore not be able to make a choice. The case against advertising is that it is an unnecessary cost that is passed on to the consumer.

What does the specification require?

It is important to understand that promotion is just one part of the marketing mix, and that it is the balance of price, product, promotion and distribution that is important. You need to show understanding of the importance of these different elements and the ways in which they can be used separately or together to influence consumer purchasing.

Questions on promotion may cover advertising, media selection and point-of-sale promotions, as well as promotional pricing. Questions are most likely to be asked in the context of advising a business.

Test yourself

Copy and complete the following sentences:

Promotion is the way a business .... customers about products and .... them to buy. Advertising is .... for a product that is paid for directly; it is therefore called .... expenditure. Advertising is used to .... products through broadcast and print .... Advertising that is not directly paid for is called .... expenditure. This includes .... such as money-off coupons and special offers.

Try this

Question based on the 'Business communication and marketing' option

PetsFirst sells a range of specialist pet foods and pet accessories via a mail order catalogue.

The range of goods sold includes specialist food for dogs, cats and caged birds; toys for dogs and cats; cage toys for budgies; collars and novelties with pet pictures, such as calendars, tea towels and place mats.

The owners have discussed the following methods of promoting the business:
- 'three for the price of two' offers (the customer buys three products and gets the cheapest one free)
- selling other products, such as cat and dog flaps and bird cages
- providing a 'satisfaction or your money back' guarantee
- providing a monthly newsletter to customers

Recommend which two of these methods would be most effective in promoting the business.

(6 marks)

Place (distribution)

Core knowledge

'Place' in the marketing mix refers both to the place where a product is sold and to how the product gets there.

The first part of this definition includes any 'place' where a customer can buy a good or service. This does not have to be a physical building such as a shop or supermarket, but can be a virtual place such as internet and catalogue buying, mail order and telephone ordering. It also includes machines such as ticket machines and drinks vending machines.

The second part of the definition is called distribution — it is concerned with how the product gets to the place where the customer can buy it, or use it. Internet sales are a growing market with many large grocery stores now offering an online ordering service backed up by home delivery.

Chain of distribution

The traditional distribution strategy was via 'long channel' distribution. This meant that the product followed a chain of distribution:

Raw material producer → Manufacturer → Wholesaler → Retailer → Consumer

The problem with such a channel is both the time it takes and the additional expense as the product passes through each **intermediary**. Businesses can use **push** or **pull strategies** to speed up progress through the chain. Shorter channels can be achieved by cutting out parts of the chain. The shortest channel is called direct supply — this is when the consumer buys direct from the producer.

Transport at each stage of the chain adds to costs

Direct sales

Some products are sold directly to customers. This is true of all personal services, which must, by definition, be delivered directly to the person. Most industrial goods, such as machinery and equipment, are sold by an agent through direct sales. Some well-known products have also taken this route. These include products such as Tupperware, which are sold by **party selling**, and Avon cosmetics, sold by door-to-door salespersons.

Place (distribution)

Retail outlets

Retail outlets range from the small corner store or convenience outlet, up to supermarkets and department stores. Many still specialise in a particular product, while others offer a general range. Outlets need to consider:

- which products will sell best
- which will give the best profit
- which they have room to stock
- which are the best-known brands

Some major retailers do not offer shelf space to more than the brand leader and their own brand. This can be a problem for products that are popular but not market leaders.

Key points

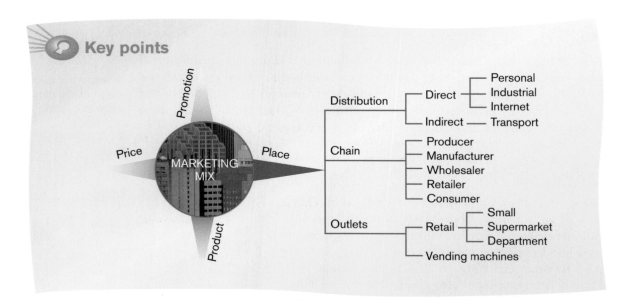

What does the specification require?

The specification refers to the traditional fourth 'P' of the marketing mix not as 'place', but as 'placement'. This is to emphasise that it is not just the place where the product is sold that is important, but the way in which the product gets to that place (or consumer) — that is, distribution and the various channels of distribution. You need to show that you understand that distribution is just one part of the marketing mix, and that it is the balance of price, product, promotion and distribution that is important. You need to show understanding of the importance of these different elements and the ways in which they can be used separately or together to influence consumer purchasing.

The 'Business communication and marketing' option looks at changes in distribution channels and how these can be of benefit to both the business and its customers.

Test yourself

Read the key terms and their definitions on the page 132, then, without looking at them, write a definition of:

➤ intermediary

➤ push strategies

➤ pull strategies

➤ party selling

Try this

Question based on the 'Business communication and marketing' option

> PetsFirst sells a range of specialist pet foods and pet accessories via a mail order catalogue.
>
> PetsFirst currently sells goods only in the UK. The company is considering whether to aim for a wider, international market. This could enable it to sell more and achieve higher profits. However, new technology might be needed to keep up with demand, and distribution costs would rise.

Advise the business on whether or not it should stay local or aim global.

(6 marks)

Test on Chapter 7

1 Which of the following is not a main source for desk research?

A books
B newspapers and journals
C questionnaires
D internet

2 Which of the following is not a feature of field research?

A It is targeted.
B It is up to date.
C It is inexpensive.
D It is time consuming.

3 The type of good that can be used again and again is called:

A a consumer good
B an industrial good
C a consumer durable
D a consumer non-durable

4 A narrow product mix means that:

A the business makes products and services
B the business makes a range of goods
C the business concentrates on a few products
D the business sells a range of services

5 Creating a memorable name or image for a product is called:

A product recognition
B targeted advertising
C product mixing
D branding

6 A product life cycle that ends because the product fails to live up to expectations is called:

A shortened
B extended
C aborted
D saturated

7 Which of the following is not a recognised part of a product life cycle?

A development
B maturity
C decline
D popularity

8 Cost-plus pricing is calculated as:

A fixed cost plus variable cost
B cost plus mark-up
C start-up cost plus variable cost
D revenue minus costs

9 Below-the-line promotion is:

A paid-for advertising
B advertising that is not paid for
C advertising that is not directly paid for
D not very effective advertising

10 The traditional channel of distribution involving manufacturers, wholesalers and retailers is called:

A short-chain
B long-chain
C complex distribution
D intermediate distribution

Chapter 8 Customers and consumers

There is a difference between 'customer' and 'consumer'. Customers are the people who actually buy a product. They may be buying it for their own use — in which case they are also the consumers. Alternatively, they may be buying it for someone else — a child, a partner, a friend. Businesses recognise this and tend to aim marketing at the consumers. For example, more men buy perfume for women than women buy for themselves. Businesses therefore target advertising at the women (the consumers), who then persuade the men (the customers) of what they want.

This distinction is important because the customer is the one who has to be happy at the point of purchase. He or she has to find the retail outlet convenient and expects good service and advice. The consumer, on the other hand, expects the products bought to be of good quality and to do what they are supposed to do. This is covered by consumer protection laws.

Customer service

Core knowledge

Businesses need to know information about their customers, including how satisfied they are with the service they are receiving. Dealing with customers is sometimes handled by a separate department within a business, although a small business, such as a sole trader, has to deal with customers directly. Customer service is used to attract customers and, more importantly, to keep them. It is much cheaper for a business to **retain** customers than it is to try to win new ones.

Good customer service is important to retain customers

STEVE MAY/ALAMY

The four important aspects of customer service are:
- providing information
- giving advice
- after-sales service
- providing convenient ways to pay

Providing information

Information can be given in a number of ways:
- by staff in a retail outlet
- by staff in a call centre or similar operation
- on websites and in other published material such as catalogues and price lists
- on the packaging of the product
- packed with the product in leaflet form

Information on packaging — to avoid allergic reactions, consumers must be advised that a product may contain nuts

Information must be accurate and provide, as a minimum, what the law requires. Information can also be provided to help buyers in other ways. Supermarkets and many other shops provide itemised bills at the checkout.

Giving advice

Advice given about a product must be accurate. It may be either printed or published, and may tell customers how to use a product safely or efficiently. Even if the advice given is verbal, it must be accurate. Customers should be able to expect to receive specialist advice if they ask a shop assistant. Asking opinions ('does this top go with this skirt?') is different from asking advice ('can I wash this in hot water?'). Customer service staff should be trained to give correct advice.

After-sales service

Sometimes after-sales service is more important than the product. If you bought a car but then found that parts for it were unavailable, the car would be fairly useless. In the case of cars and some other products, after-sales service extends for years after purchase. In other cases, it may involve nothing more than a delivery service, or the wrapping of the product once it is bought. After-sales also deals with complaints, refunds and exchanges.

Speak the language

eftpos — stands for 'electronic funds transfer at point of sale', when a number is keyed into a pad at a point of sale

retain — meaning to 'keep'; in customer service the technical term is 'customer retention'

Providing convenient ways to pay

It is in the interest of the business to make payment as convenient as possible. Many businesses therefore provide multiple ways to pay, such as credit, hire purchase and cash. They may also choose to accept credit and debit cards and to use electronic (**eftpos**) keypads for transactions.

Key points

Information	• accurate
	• helpful
	• clear
Advice	• accurate
	• specialist
	• as required
After-sales	• delivery
	• packaging
	• warranties
Ways to pay	• cash
	• credit/debit cards

What does the specification require?

Questions on the topics covered in this section — customers and consumers — might be asked on the core paper, but knowledge of these topics is more likely to be required for tackling parts of other questions. You might be asked about customers, for example, as part of a number of stakeholder groups, or about the idea of customer satisfaction linked with quality products and services. You might be asked to describe how a business could respond to the needs of its customers, although how it finds out about those needs is covered in marketing. You should also know how a business behaves towards both customers and competitors (and other stakeholders, such as communities) in a competitive market.

The 'Business communication and marketing' option covers different forms of credit, their use in marketing and the way in which consumers can be protected from misuse. You need to understand why legislation and voluntary and industry controls are necessary to protect the consumer and how such legislation and controls work. Questions will not ask you for specifics of Acts or dates.

The specification recognises that, to succeed, a business needs to offer good customer service, which has been the subject of this section. This is especially true in competitive markets, as efficiency in gaining and retaining customers will make a business more competitive. As indicated above, you are unlikely to be asked direct questions about customer service, but might bring in this knowledge as part of answers to other questions, such as on the idea of 'quality' or in terms of marketing or training.

The 'Business communication and marketing option' covers customer service in greater detail — for instance, in studying how information and assistance may be given to customers as part of a general marketing strategy.

Test yourself

Link each of the following terms to one of the four aspects of customer service — information, advice, after-sales and ways to pay:

- accurate
- as required
- specialist
- delivery
- credit cards
- helpful
- cash
- packaging
- clear
- warranties

Try this

Question based on the 'Business communication and marketing' option

PetsFirst sells a range of specialist pet foods and pet accessories via a mail order catalogue.

Suggest three ways in which PetsFirst could give information to its customers. Explain why giving information is important. **(5 marks)**

Measuring customer satisfaction

The number of returns is a quantitative measure of customer satisfaction

Core knowledge

Good customer service is vital to a business, both for attracting new customers and for keeping its current ones. A business must therefore have some way to measure whether service is effective. It needs to know if customers are happy. This can be done through measurements of customer satisfaction.

Quantitative measurements

Businesses may be able to measure satisfaction by counting. They can, for example, count how many goods are returned, or how many complaints they receive. Such **quantitative measurements** are just a first step in providing an overview. It is more important to know if returns continued after action was taken to correct a fault, or the nature of complaints. Businesses can also count positive actions such as how many customers return or introduce a friend.

Qualitative measurements

Satisfaction is not something that can always be measured in numbers. Customers will have an opinion on the quality of product and support that they should be getting. This can be assessed using **qualitative measurements**. One way to find out if customers are happy is to ask them. Businesses do this in various ways — through questionnaires, feedback forms on websites, questions on order forms, guarantees and competition entries.

Setting targets

Finding out what pleases or annoys customers is a first step to measuring satisfaction. For example, if customers don't like being put on hold, businesses will work to keep this to a minimum. They may set targets that they can measure, such as 'no customer to be on hold for more than 1 minute'.

Guarantees

Customer satisfaction guarantees are provided with many products. These say that if a customer is not happy with a product, he or she can return it. This goes further than the law, which says that a good can be returned or a service is unacceptable only if it is not a 'quality' product: that is, if it does not do what it is supposed to do. (Quality is defined on page 109.)

Value added

A successful business is one where customers think they are getting value for money. Value can be added to a good or service through the customer service that goes with it. In some cases, this can be even more important than price, and can persuade customers to stay with a business.

> ### Speak the language
>
> **qualitative measurements** — measurements that involve thoughts and opinions
>
> **quantitative measurements** — measurements that involve quantity (numbers)

Customers don't like to be kept hanging on

IKON/CADMIUM

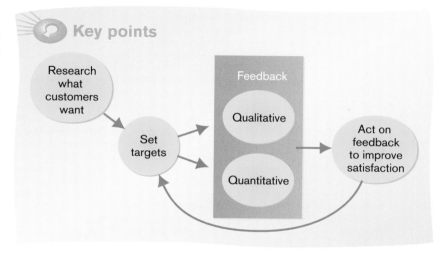

Key points

Research what customers want → Set targets → Feedback (Qualitative / Quantitative) → Act on feedback to improve satisfaction

Measuring customer satisfaction

What does the specification require?

The measurement of customer satisfaction is often included in marketing and market research-type questions. It might also be included in questions about business objectives. For example, a particular level of customer service (always answering the phone within three rings; dealing with customer queries within 7 days) might be an aim or target of a business.

Test yourself

Without looking at the key points on page 139, copy and complete the following diagram to summarise how businesses measure customer satisfaction.

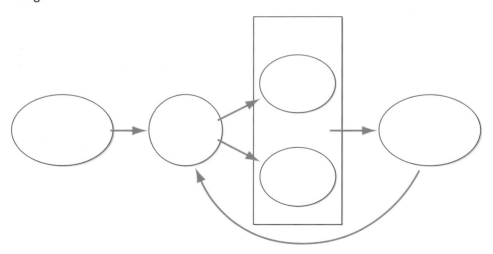

Try this

Alternative paper to coursework question

Royaume Ltd is a worldwide business, specialising in sports equipment, clothing and shoes.

Explain two ways in which market research can help a business such as Royaume to improve its levels of customer satisfaction. **(6 marks)**

Consumer protection

Core knowledge

Sometimes businesses try to cheat customers, or deny them their rights. To counter this, the government passes laws to protect the consumer. By law, products bought should be:

- as described
- **fit for purpose**
- not faulty or dangerous

Businesses should treat consumers fairly; this includes being clear about charges and penalties, and using accurate weights and measures.

Consumers should find six large, free-range eggs inside this box

The consumer

In the UK, the first line of consumer defence is the consumer. A consumer is expected to take care to buy the right product for the purpose and to read, understand and follow any instructions. The Latin tag for this is **caveat emptor** — let the buyer beware.

Laws

The main laws protecting consumers from harm and from being cheated are as follows:

Food and Drugs Act
- Businesses must not sell goods that are 'unfit for human consumption'.
- Labels must be accurate.

Trades Descriptions Act
- Accurate descriptions of goods must be given wherever they are described, including in advertising.

Consumer Credit Act
- Full information regarding the costs of credit purchases must be clearly given, including the costs of interest and the actual price that will be paid.
- A **cooling-off period** is allowed for credit that is arranged outside business premises (e.g. in the home).

Consumer Protection Act
- Sale prices must be genuine.
- Goods that may be harmful or dangerous must be labelled as such.

> ### Speak the language
>
> **caveat emptor** — let the buyer beware; consumers should always take care
>
> **cooling-off period** — this gives consumers time to rethink if they have been persuaded to accept a deal
>
> **fit for purpose** — a good should do what it is supposed to do (see 'quality', page 109)

Sale of Goods Acts and Supply of Goods and Services Act
- Goods must be of a satisfactory quality to be sold.
- Goods must fulfil the purpose for which they are sold.
- Consumers are entitled to replacements or refunds.
- In the case of a service not being properly carried out, consumers should receive a refund or a correct service charged to the original business.

Local government

Inspectors are employed by local government to check hygiene in places preparing, serving or selling food, and to check the accuracy of weights and measures being used.

Independent help

Some consumer protection exists outside the law. The main instruments are:
- industry bodies, such as the British Electro-Technical Approvals Board for electrical items
- the British Standards Institute, which tests and approves products and awards the BSI 'kite mark'
- Which?, formerly the Consumers' Association, acting on behalf of consumers, and testing and reporting on products

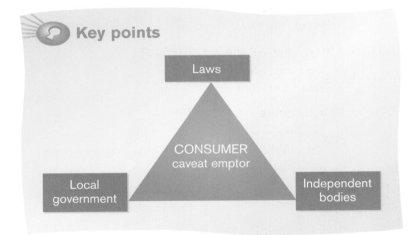

Key points

Laws

CONSUMER
caveat emptor

Local government

Independent bodies

Boost your grade

You are unlikely to be asked for a specific date for a law. Even if you can't remember the exact name of a law, this does not matter as long as you can talk about what consumer law is basically for, and some of its main features.

What does the specification require?

Consumer protection appears in a number of sections in the specification. It is recognised as one of the 'Influences on business activity' in the section on 'Aiding and controlling business activity' and as a key element in e-commerce transactions. In the 'Business communication and marketing' option, you should know how customer protection may be seen as a constraint on marketing activities, how and why legislation is used, and about other constraints. These include restrictions on advertising (such as timing, honesty, banned products and false claims) and the role of key organisations such as the Advertising Standards Authority (ASA), the Independent Television Commission (ITC) and Which?.

Test yourself

1 Reasons why government passes laws to protect the consumer include all of the following except:

 A Some business try to cheat customers
 B Some businesses may deny customers their rights
 C Some products may be faulty
 D Some products may be fit for purpose

2 Businesses should, when dealing with customers, do all of the following except:

 A Treat customers fairly   C Deny customers rights
 B Use accurate weights   D Clearly show charges

3 In UK consumer law, it is the responsibility of which of the following to make sure that the product is what they want:

 A Businesses   C Consumers
 B Government   D British standards Institute

4 Food that is 'unfit for human consumption' is covered under which Act?

 A Food and Drugs Act   C Consumer Credit Act
 B Consumer Protection Act   D Trades Descriptions Act

5 The accuracy of advertising claims is covered under which Act?

 A Food and Drugs Act   C Consumer Credit Act
 B Consumer Protection Act   D Trades Descriptions Act

Try this

Core paper question

Recently, a customer bought a hair dye product from Sarah's shop, and did not ask for any advice about the product. The customer is now demanding her money back, as the colour did not match the outfit she had bought. 'It ruined my evening,' she explained, 'and I think I should be compensated.'

Explain the customer's rights in this situation. How would you advise Sarah with regard to this customer?   **(6 marks)**

Test on Chapter 8

1 Which of the following is not one of the main parts of customer service?

A providing information
B giving advice
C after-sales service
D packing customers' bags

2 The missing major aspect of customer service in question 1 is:

A delivery
B putting up a website
C providing convenient ways to pay
D being polite

3 The most important feature of customer information on a product is that it is:

A prominent
B accurate
C detailed
D printed

4 All products bought should be quality products — that is, they should be:

A expensive
B exclusive
C fit for purpose
D delivered

5 Eftpos stands for:

A electronic funds transfer at point of shopping
B electric funds to at process of shopping
C electronic funds transfer at point of sale
D electric funds transfer at place of sale

6 According to the Food and Drugs Act, businesses must not sell food that:

A is not very fresh
B is packaged in plastic
C is unfit for human consumption
D has reached its 'sell by' date

7 'Caveat emptor' is the Latin tag that means:

A let the buyer beware
B let the seller be careful
C the price is right
D the cave is empty

8 Measurements of consumer satisfaction that involve thoughts and opinions are called:

A qualitative
B quantitative
C questionable
D questionnaires

9 A period during which a consumer can pull out of a credit deal is called a:

A cooling-off period
B credit open period
C customer withdrawal period
D customer credit period

10 The 'kite mark' is the mark of quality applied by the:

A Basic Standards Institute
B British Standards Institute
C British Sanitary Institute
D Basic Standards Institution

Chapter 9
Issues in business

This chapter covers some of the current issues and ideas that are affecting business. Many of these do not fit neatly into other chapters, but are issues that are likely to have some effect on all businesses, from the largest down to the smallest sole trader. Whatever a business sells, at least some of it is likely to have originated abroad, so international trade and whether or not it is fair will affect most businesses.

Many businesses are also keen to show that they are operating in a responsible way, particularly with regard to the environment, so want to buy products that have been grown or made in a sustainable way. This is important to the business in two ways: first, in establishing a good reputation and, second, in attracting those customers — an increasingly large number — who are keen to buy goods and services of this type.

E-commerce was covered briefly in 'The role of ICT' in Chapter 3, but it is something that all businesses should be aware of and, if possible, should use to enhance their revenue and profits. Therefore, it is examined in more detail here.

E-commerce and the internet

Core knowledge

E-commerce has become a major way for businesses to trade. It refers to buying and selling goods or services over the internet. Usually it involves a website and a means of ordering and paying electronically. Businesses can operate in one of two ways:

- as pure 'dotcom' companies (e.g. Dell), with no physical shops or other outlets; or
- as **'bricks and clicks'** operations, having both websites and high-street premises (e.g. Tesco)

There is still a lot of growth in e-commerce to go. There are now over a billion users of the internet worldwide, but this represents only around a sixth of the world's population. The biggest growth markets are China, Africa and Asia.

Business expansion

For small and medium-sized businesses there are two main possibilities for expansion on the internet. These are **B2C** and **B2B** — business to consumer and business to business. While the rate of growth has slowed down in both sectors, it is still taking place. In addition, there is a third growing market: business to government, or **B2G**. To encourage small businesses, government help in the form of advice and information is available at **www.businesslink. gov.uk**.

Google is one of the most popular search engines

Good and bad websites

Businesses cannot just put up a website and hope customers will come calling. They need to advertise it (using traditional media) and make sure that it is registered on **search engines**. The key differences between good and poor websites are shown on page 147.

Laws

Websites are governed by the same consumer laws as shops. Goods and services must still be 'as described' and 'fit for purpose', and can be returned if they are not. The government has drawn up special distance selling regulations for websites and others who sell 'remotely' — that is, over the phone or via catalogues.

New technology

Businesses need to learn to take advantage of new technologies to keep costs low. For instance, new internet technology is allowing more broadband to be provided. On the back of this, new VOIP (voice over internet protocol) connections are allowing phone calls, even international ones, to be made virtually free.

Speak the language

bricks and clicks — operations with both websites and physical premises

B2B — selling from business to business

B2C — selling from business to consumer

B2G — selling from business to government

search engines — programs that search for websites using key words

 Key points

Websites can have good points and bad points.

Good points	Bad points
• Customers can find it easily	• Difficult to find
• Customers can find their way around (navigate) easily	• Difficult to read (because of choice of fonts or an over-complex page design)
• Easy to read	• Not secure
• Safe and secure	• Hard to navigate
• Reliable	

Boost your grade

The classic answer to business questions about the use of the internet, e-commerce and other e-media is that they are 'cheap, quick and easy'. However, this is not enough. You should try to think of a specific way in which the technology is helping a business, and about issues such as the cost of initial set-up or of training staff.

What does the specification require?

The specification emphasises the issues raised in Chapter 9 through its concern with 'Business and change'. It sees areas of 'new' business, such as e-commerce and the opportunities presented by Europe, as important. There is a core section on 'The changing business environment' and both options cover ideas in this section.

'Business and change' looks at the way both the business and economic environments change, and how businesses can manage or gain from such changes. These include new technology, Europe and international trade.

'Business communication and marketing' puts particular emphasis on the impact of e-commerce on business activity.

You need to be able to explain the ways in which technology, such as information technology and e-commerce, have had an impact on business, and how businesses are coping with changes.

The impact of e-commerce is given a whole section in the 'Business communication and marketing' option. You need to be able to define and explain the nature of e-commerce, identify the pressures on businesses to adopt it, and understand the difficulties in developing e-commerce. Within a business context, you may be asked to evaluate the benefits and threats of e-commerce to both customers and businesses, particularly in the areas of security and confidentiality.

The 'Marketing and the business environment' option looks at e-commerce from the angle of how it may be used by a business to aid promotion and develop brand and customer loyalty.

Test yourself

Read the key terms and their definitions on page 146, then, without looking at them, write a definition of:

➤ 'bricks and clicks'   ➤ B2C   ➤ B2B

➤ search engines   ➤ B2G

Try this

Question based on the 'Business communication and marketing' option

> PetsFirst sells a range of specialist pet foods and pet accessories via a mail order catalogue. The company is considering setting up a website to sell products over the internet.

Explain the problems that both PetsFirst and its customers could face if the company sells goods over the internet.   **(6 marks)**

The European Union

Core knowledge

The European Union (EU) is a group of countries in Europe that have agreed to act together on a number of issues, many of which affect business. It provides businesses within the union with a larger market (the **single European market**) of over 360 million people. At the time of writing it has 27 member states and stretches from Sweden and Finland in the north to Malta and Greece in the south, from Portugal and Spain in the west to Latvia and Estonia in the east. It is a powerful **trading bloc** that other countries (currently Turkey, Bulgaria and Romania) are keen to join.

The euro

Europe has moved towards **harmonisation** of measurements, laws and even currency. The countries of the EU decided that it would be much easier for businesses and trade in general if they were all using the same currency. This single currency, the euro, was introduced in 1999. It is beneficial to business (and overseas travellers) because the charges and confusion that go with currency changes are avoided. It has also made trade easier and smoother as prices quoted in a common currency are better understood by all trading parties. However, not all countries have joined the euro. The UK, for instance, has said it will not join until certain economic conditions have been met.

The Maastricht Treaty

The Maastricht Treaty of 1991 was designed to encourage all member states to work within the same rules. It included the **Social Chapter**, which promoted:

- the right of workers to join a trade union
- the right to equal treatment for men and women at work
- more worker involvement in businesses through worker councils
- a minimum wage
- maximum working hours
- freedom for EU citizens to work in any EU country

Speak the language

harmonisation — making conditions and regulations the same in all member countries

single European market — within EU borders, where goods and labour are free to move as if there were no borders

Social Chapter — the part of the Maastricht Treaty dealing with issues such as workers' rights; countries could choose to bring in changes gradually

trading bloc — a collection of countries that gain power by trading as one group, e.g. the European Union

Current members of the European Union

Year of joining EU

- 1958
- 1973
- 1981
- 1986
- 1995
- 2004
- 2007
- Applicant country

EU policies

Some of the main policies to affect business are as follows:

- *Common Agricultural Policy*. This policy was introduced to help farmers by guaranteeing prices. If too much of a crop is produced, the EU buys up the excess in order to prevent prices falling. This keeps prices artificially high, but helps farmers.
- *European Regional Policy*. This helps those regions of the EU where traditional industry has declined and where unemployment is high. Regional funding is also available to help develop transport and services.
- *European Social Fund*. This pays for the retraining of workers and for programmes to regenerate industry.

Key points

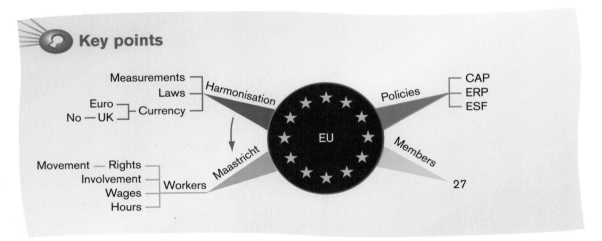

What does the specification require?

In the core part of the specification, you need to be able to explain the importance of the single European market and to demonstrate the main ways in which the role of the UK within the EU affects the business environment. You also need to know about the good and bad points of a single European currency and the reasons why the UK has opted out of it. This is also included in the 'Business and change' option.

Test yourself

Read the key terms and definitions on page 149 then, without looking at them, write a definition of:

➤ European Union
➤ Social Chapter

➤ single European market
➤ trading bloc

Try this

Core paper question

Fiveways Farm Ltd is a large dairy farm. It produces milk, cream and cheese, and has recently gone into making bio-yoghurts. Dan Farrer owns Fiveways. Dan sells his yoghurts in the UK and other EU countries.

Explain how Dan may have benefited from EU 'harmonisation' and the introduction of the euro.

(6 marks)

International trade and globalisation

Core knowledge

International trade allows businesses to exchange goods that they can produce with those that businesses in other countries can produce. This benefits both parties as long as production takes place in the country that is relatively more efficient at producing that particular product. **Globalisation** describes the movement of businesses towards operating on a worldwide basis. Some businesses make a point of focusing on global markets rather than on local ones. Coca-Cola, for instance, has expanded not just into Europe, but also into Africa, China and Russia. It wants a majority share of the global market for soft drinks, not just the home market.

Without international trade, many of the products that we take for granted would not be available to us

International trade

International trade is made up of two distinct types of product, moving in two directions. The types of product are:

- **visibles** — goods that can be seen or touched
- **invisibles** — services such as insurance or transport, which cannot be seen or touched

The products move either into or out of a country:

- Imports are products brought into a country from abroad.
- Exports are products sold to countries abroad.

INGRAM

International trade and globalisation

Speak the language

globalisation — the movement of businesses towards operating in world markets

invisibles — trade in services

multinationals — businesses with bases in several different countries

visibles — international trade in goods

Exchange rates

Such trade also involves currency exchanges. A car bought from the USA will need to be paid for in dollars, so the number of dollars to the pound is an important factor in determining price. For example, if you import a $150,000 car from the USA to the UK and the exchange rate was $1.5 to £1 then you would need £100,000 to buy the necessary dollars. If the exchange rate was $2 to £1 you would then only need £75,000.

Multinationals

Many companies that operate on a global basis are **multinationals**. They have factories and operations in many countries. This allows them to move their investments and profits to keep their costs and taxation low. They may be able to take advantage of lower labour costs, or less organised labour. This has brought globalisation into conflict with human rights groups, which see global businesses as exploiting labour and natural resources in poorer countries in order to boost profits in richer ones. While some people criticise multinationals for this, others congratulate them for bringing work to poorer countries.

Global branding

A global brand is where the same good or service, with the same qualities and reputation, is available around the globe. Sometimes this may require a name change, as in the case of the 'Marathon' bar, which became 'Snickers' in the UK to match its international name. But more often than not, global brands are linked to particular images or lifestyles.

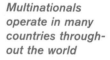

Multinationals operate in many countries throughout the world

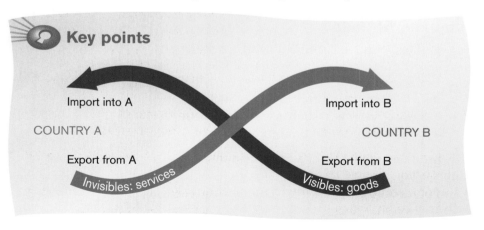

Key points

Import into A

COUNTRY A

Export from A

Invisibles: services

Import into B

COUNTRY B

Export from B

Visibles: goods

> ## Boost your grade
>
> If in doubt about whether a good or service is an import or an export, think about which way the money has gone. Whichever way payment went, the product went the other way.
>
> For example, in the case of a US tourist in London paying for a hotel room, the payment is from the USA to the UK, while the service (tourism) has gone from the UK to the USA. This is an invisible export.

What does the specification require?

You need to be able to explain how increased world trade can influence the UK economy. In particular, you should know how it creates opportunities for growth but also places greater pressure on certain industries through increased competition.

In the 'Business and change' option, you need to know about the factors influencing the level of international trade and about the effects of changing exchange rates.

Test yourself

1 If you were in the UK, a sale of cars to the USA would be:

A a visible export
B an invisible import

C a visible import
D an invisible export

2 If you lived in the UK and hired a car while on holiday in the USA, to the US economy this would be:

A a visible export
B an invisible import

C a visible import
D an invisible export

3 If you lived in the USA and bought a flight from Air France, this would be:

A a visible export
B an invisible import

C a visible import
D an invisible export

4 If you lived in the UK and hired a car while on holiday in the USA, to the UK economy this would be:

A a visible export
B an invisible import

C a visible import
D an invisible export

5 If you lived in the UK and bought goods from a US website, to the UK economy this would be:

A a visible export
B an invisible import

C a visible import
D an invisible export

Try this

Question based on the 'Business and change' option

> Merrion's Garage Services Ltd is a private limited company owned by John Merrion and his family. It recently bought 20 cars from German manufacturers to sell in the UK. The price quoted was £8,000 per car or €10,000. The exchange rate at the time was is €1 = 70p.

What price would you have advised them to take? Explain why.   **(3 marks)**

Fair trade

Core knowledge

Although international trade is essential for providing countries with many of the goods and services that they require — and that they have become used to — such trade is not always seen as being fair. Many organisations think that international trade does not give a fair deal to many poorer countries, but actually exploits them. More established businesses, in **developed nations**, are able to take advantage of their market strength to keep newer competitor countries out of world markets.

Protection

Some countries protect industry from competition. To do this they can use various methods:

- tariffs — taxes on goods entering a country
- quotas — limiting imports to a certain number
- subsidies — making home produce cheaper
- special regulations — rules that make it harder to import

Emerging nations may not be strong enough to compete straight away without some sort of protection, but it is generally accepted that the less protection there is, the better this is for trade.

What is fair trade?

Free trade is the term usually used to refer to a reduction in tariffs, duties and other restrictions, all of which add to the costs of international trade and therefore increase the price of

products. **Fair trade** refers to how and when these restrictions can be reduced without harming smaller nations. However, there is still debate as to whether removing these protections will in fact make poorer countries worse off. The World Trade Organization, in a series of talks that have taken place over several years, is trying to make trade fair for all, but even countries like the USA feel that some of their markets need to be protected.

The problem is that, in making trade fairer for emerging nations, established ones may lose out and damage their own industries, and they do not wish to do this.

Fair trade is also involved with human rights. Many countries do not want to trade with nations that have poor human rights records, or which are shown to be damaging the environment in order to make profits. The other side of the argument is that such countries may not be able to compete if they do not pay low wages or use up natural resources.

Rainforest destruction allows for farms and trade — but at what cost?

Boost your grade

Fair trade is an area where you can show your understanding about an issue by weighing up the good and bad points and then coming to a conclusion. Whether you think that global trade is fair or not does not matter — there is no right answer. What will gain you marks is supporting your opinion with arguments.

Key points

Weigh up the arguments. Who benefits from fair trade?

- Bigger countries, from cheaper labour and lower-cost production?
- Smaller countries, from outside help and new markets?
- Consumers, from cheaper goods and better availability?
- Everyone, from freer trade?
- No one: rich countries just get richer and poor ones poorer?

What does the specification require?

The idea of fair trade has become increasingly important, but is still only a small part of business — and then only of businesses, usually larger ones, that trade internationally. Questions related to moral, ethical, social and cultural issues that affect businesses may be asked. In the 'Business communication and marketing' option, areas that are highlighted include safety features, the ethics of testing products on animals and the use and control of toxic materials and waste.

Test yourself

Match each of the following terms with its correct definition.

1 subsidy	**a** a tax on goods entering a country
2 tariff	**b** when imports are limited to a certain number
3 special regulations	**c** when home-produced goods are made cheaper
4 quota	**d** rules that make it harder to import

Try this

Alternative paper to coursework question

> Royaume Ltd is a worldwide business, specialising in sports equipment, clothing and shoes. It has operations all around the globe, including the European Union, North and South America, Asia and the Far East. Royaume operates a 'fair trade' policy. It tries to buy locally sourced materials and makes sure that some of the profits from its operations are ploughed back into the countries where it works.

Explain the advantages and disadvantages of fair trade to:

(a) emerging nations
(b) established trading nations   **(6 marks)**

Test on Chapter 9

Answer this question as fully as possible.

Extract from a case study

> Royaume Ltd is a worldwide business, specialising in sports equipment, clothing and shoes. Its head office is in Tinnerton, a new town about 25 kilometres from London, but it has operations all around the globe, including other EU countries, North and South America, Asia and the Far East. Royaume operates a 'fair trade' policy. It tries to buy locally sourced

materials and makes sure that some of the profits from its operations are ploughed back into the countries where it works.

Some of the ethical credentials of Royaume were damaged last year by an advertising campaign. Its Zipfast range of shoes had a graffiti-like logo which Muslim commentators pointed out spelt an Arabic word that was an insult to their religion. The advertisement for the Zipfast range claimed that the product would help customers to run faster and recover from effort more quickly. These were claims that the business was unable to back up.

(a) Explain what is meant by 'ethical constraints'.   (4 marks)
(b) Explain how Royaume may have breached these constraints and recommend what action it should take.   (6 marks)
(c) Explain how the actions of the business might be seen as unethical.   (2 marks)

Answers

Chapter 1

Business context

Test yourself (page 4)

Check your answers against the key terms on page 2.

Try this (page 4)

Higher interest rates will make Dan's borrowing more expensive, so he might need to put up prices. It might also mean that his customers have less money to spend, so do not buy as many of his products. However, this is unlikely to be the case with items such as yoghurt and milk, as they are not items of large expenditure for a household. If the yoghurts were considered to be luxury items, then demand could fall as people cut back on luxury spending.

Functional areas of business

Try this (page 8)

Some possible tasks are recruiting (human resources), finance and marketing (sales and marketing) and administration.

Sarah will not be able to do everything herself, so she will probably need to employ people — for example, Saturday staff for busy times and an accountant to do the books. This means that she will need to advertise for staff and interview.

Staff will need to be paid — a job for the finance area — and materials will need to be ordered and paid for.

Sarah will also need to carry out marketing to let people know that her business is open.

There will also be administrative tasks such as keeping staff records and drawing up contracts.

The operation of markets

Test yourself (page 11)

- When the demand for bread falls, the price of bread *falls*.
- When the import price of wheat rises, the price of bread *rises*.
- When bread is promoted as a healthy product, the price of bread *rises* (because demand rises).
- When farmers have a bumper crop of wheat, too much supply could lead to a *fall* in the price of bread.
- When a new brand of bread is promoted, although the new brand might be cheaper, this would probably have no effect on the market, so the price of bread *stays the same*.

Try this (page 11)

(a)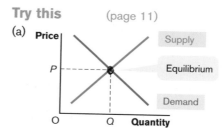

(b) Demand will fall, causing the demand curve to move to the left. This means that PetsFirst will sell fewer products at current prices or have to lower prices to sell the same amount of products.

Test on Chapter 1 (page 12)

1 A	2 B	3 B	4 D	5 B
6 D	7 C	8 C	9 B	10 D

Chapter 2

Sole traders and partnerships

Test yourself (page 16)

Advantages
- It is easy to set up.
- Responsibility is shared.
- A partner may bring fresh ideas or different skills.
- Workload is shared.

Disadvantages
- Partners may fall out.
- It would have unlimited liability.
- The business has no separate legal existence.
- The decisions of any one partner are binding on the others.

Try this (page 17)

The main benefits of being a sole trader are that it is easy to set up, one person makes all the decisions and that person keeps all the profits. The main benefits of partnerships are the ability to bring in additional expertise, shared decision making and responsibility, and extra capital. Any explanation of what would be the 'right' decision for Sarah should be backed by comment about the possible levels of risk and reward and could refer to the disadvantages of each business structure. There is no 'right' answer (as is often the case in business studies). Marks are awarded for judgements that are well argued and supported by evidence.

Limited liability companies

Test yourself (page 19)

This is a business that is incorporated, meaning that it has a separate existence from its owners. The business is owned by shareholders. Shareholders' liability for debt is limited to the amount they have risked in the business. This is called limited liability. Shares are sold to the general public and quoted on a stock exchange. Marks and Spencer plc is an example of a public limited company.

Try this (page 19)

One advantage is that a limited company would have limited liability, meaning that the owners would only be responsible for debt up to the amount they have

contributed. Many of John Merrion's liabilities will actually be covered by insurance. In addition, John and his family can sell the business on if they want to — they could not do this if it was not incorporated (i.e. a company).

Franchises

Test yourself (page 21)

| 1 B | 2 A | 3 C | 4 D | 5 D |

Try this (page 22)

Franchisers charge a fee for buying the franchise and also a royalty based on turnover. This means that there is a continuing commitment to pay the franchiser and this can be expensive. Franchisers might also be quite strict about what the franchisee is and is not allowed to do or sell. On the other hand, the franchisee is buying into a successful business, is unlikely to fail, and will receive a lot of support from the franchiser in terms of training, advertising and marketing.

Note The higher-level marks are for the strength of your argument, rather than the recommendation itself.

Multinationals and holding companies

Test yourself (page 24)

Check your answers against the key terms on page 23.

Try this (page 25)

In the case of Royaume Ltd, the use of holding companies has been a way for the founding family to retain control of the business. By launching various other companies, Royaume has been able to raise capital via stock markets. It is also able to dispose of any companies that it no longer wants — either because they are now worth selling, or because they are not performing well.

By keeping Royaume Ltd as a private limited company, the founders have kept control and made sure that shareholders cannot interfere with the running of the business. By keeping a majority shareholding in each subsidiary, they have the benefit of control alongside the advantages brought by being a plc.

Public sector businesses

Test yourself (page 28)

| 1 B | 2 D | 3 E | 4 A | 5 C |

The public sector is that part of the economy that is owned or managed by government (local or national) on behalf of the public. The public cannot buy shares in such businesses, which should operate for the public good rather than for profitability.

Cooperatives, charities and voluntary groups

Test yourself (page 30)

1 D   2 E   3 B   4 D   5 C

Try this   (page 31)

(a) A producer cooperative is where a number of producers — like the farms — share costs, machinery and expertise.

(b) The farms pool their money to buy, for example, one expensive machine. Each of the six farms then has access to the machine at only one-sixth of the cost. They might also share transport and a selling space at a market. They will benefit from lower costs, from having access to better machinery and from increased power in the market.

Test on Chapter 2   (page 31)

1 sole trader
2 two or more
3 Deed of Partnership
4 Liability
5 two
6 Memorandum of Association
7 Certificate of Incorporation
8 public sector
9 franchiser
10 floating
11 expand
12 royalty
13 mutual society
14 holding company
15 multinational *or* transnational
16 watchdog
17 taxation
18 Charities
19 worker cooperative
20 franchisee

Chapter 3

Enterprise and management

Test yourself (page 36)

Check your answers against the key terms on page 34.

Try this   (page 36)

The profit could be seen as a reward for enterprise, so John Merrion and his family could pay it to themselves — as shareholders in a private limited company — in dividends. It might also be ploughed back into the business: for instance, to buy new stock or equipment. It could be used to motivate workers by having profitability linked to bonus payments. Some of it might be used to pay taxation, or saved for future projects or problems.

Stakeholders

Test yourself (page 39)

Look at the diagram on page 38 to see if you have included all the groups and individuals, and have correctly identified internal and external stakeholders.

Try this   (page 39)

Possible stakeholders that you could name include owners, employees, managers, customers, suppliers, communities, government, foreign governments, bankers and contractors. Reasons for their interest in the business could include:

- Communities — to know that employment is being provided; to know that the business is putting something back into the community; to know that the business is not causing problems such as pollution.
- Employees — to make sure that jobs and incomes are safeguarded; to make sure Royaume is a success, so that they can share in that success with better wages, pensions etc.
- Bankers — to make sure that their money is being used efficiently; to know that they can be repaid.
- Government — to check that rules, regulations and laws are being upheld; to collect taxation; needs employment and exports to be provided.

Business aims and objectives

Test yourself (page 41)

1 A   2 B   3 B   4 D   5 A

Try this   (page 42)

Jeb's business will be new, so his main objective in the first year should be to survive. He can do this by being efficient and by building up a good customer base. To survive he should aim at least to break even, which means that he should take as much in revenue as he spends in costs. A further aim could be to make a profit.

However, in the first year of a new business, this is not as important as establishing a good customer base and a good reputation on which Jeb can build in the future.

Business organisation

Test yourself (page 46)

Check your answers against the key terms on page 45.

Try this (page 46)

(a) Three

(b) This means the breadth of someone's control. For example, the garage manager's span (three areas) is wider than that of the administration supervisor (two areas).

Business size and growth

Test yourself (page 49)

Look at page 47 to check your table is correct.

Try this (page 49)

(a) If a business diversifies, it moves into areas other than its core area.

(b) A merger involves agreement between two parties; an acquisition means that one business buys out another.

(c) As is often the case in business, there is no 'right' answer. It is the reasons that you give which will gain you marks. Acquiring a rival garage would reduce competition and give Merrion's a larger market share; it could also produce economies of scale. Diversification would enable Merrion's to try new markets for which it might need new expertise. This could be costly, but could also help the rest of the business. A merger would bring economies of scale, but Merrion's could lose control of the business if the car showroom is the 'senior' partner.

Management styles

Test yourself (page 52)

1 B   2 C   3 D   4 A

Try this (page 52)

(a) Asif has an authoritarian or autocratic management style. This is shown in his lack of consultation, his insistence on having set tasks and checks, and his imposition of strict systems on the running of the business.

(b) One disadvantage of this approach is that it might upset some employees if they are not consulted, as has happened with the farm workers. This might make them less willing to work and carry out the tasks set. It also assumes that the manager's way is the only way, even though it may not be the most efficient and does not use the experience or expertise of the workers.

Communication

Test yourself (page 54)

Internal communications take place within a business. **External** communications take place between businesses and other groups. They may be in a set format, called **formal** communications, or can take place outside a framework, called **informal** communications. The originator of communication is the **sender**, who sends the message through a particular way, or **medium**. An important part of the process is that the **receiver** provides **feedback** to show that the message has been understood.

Try this (page 55)

Answers should refer to the factors that act as barriers to good communication. Calls were at what, for many, would be an antisocial time, the nature of the call might not have been made clear, and phone communication might not have been the most effective method for such a long survey.

The role of ICT

Test yourself (page 58)

1C   2 F   3 E   4 D   5 B   6 A

Try this (page 58)

Communication — could be through electronic data transmission such as e-mail. This would be cheaper than other methods and can be targeted, but the information sent would probably be limited.

Record keeping — PetsFirst could keep records on databases, allowing it also to send out standard letters or e-mails to specific customer groups. A database would let it know who buys what, and therefore what other products it could sell to them.

Finance — spreadsheets could be used for customers' accounts, for calculations on accounts and for providing financial forecasts.

Marketing — various ICT applications could be used. For example, desktop publishing packages could be used to create leaflets and catalogues, e-mail could be used to communicate special offers and databases could be used for mailshots.

Test on Chapter 3 (page 59)

1 A	2 C	3 B	4 C	5 D
6 B	7 B	8 C	9 B	10 C

Chapter 4
Sources of finance

Test yourself (page 63)

Look at the table on page 61 to check your answers.

Try this (page 63)

(a) Owners' funds are the money earned or saved by John that he is willing to put into the business; a bank loan is for the medium or long term, and is usually secured against something valuable; an overdraft is permission to take extra money from a current account.

(b) John may not have had enough of his own money, so needed to borrow. The different forms of borrowing used will depend on what the money is for and how long it is needed. An overdraft tends to be short-term and more flexible, and may be unsecured. A loan is usually longer-term and secured.

Costs and revenue

Test yourself (page 65)

1 C	2 D	3 B	4 A	5 D

Try this (page 66)

Revenue is calculated as sales × price. In this case, it is:

$(40 \times £50) + (118 \times £12) + (132 \times £60)$

$= £2,000 + £1,416 + £7,920 = £11,336$

Note You will lose marks if you do not show your working or include '£' signs.

Breaking even

Test yourself (page 68)

Check your answers against the complete diagram on page 67

Try this (page 69)

(a) Fixed costs include rent, rates, interest payments and the monthly fees for telephones, utilities etc. Variable costs are those that are specific to the operation. In this example, they could be the water and power used and materials such as lotions and setting solutions.

(b) Contribution per item is £25 − £15 = £10

Breakeven is £20,000/£10 = 2,000

Marks awarded for: 25 **(1)** minus **(1)** 15 **(1)** = 10 **(1)**; 20,000 **(1)** divided by/over **(1)** 10 **(1)** = 2,000 **(1)**. A total of 8 marks for a straightforward calculation.

Financial documents

Test yourself (page 71)

Businesses use a **purchase order** to say what they want to buy, how much they want and what they expect to pay. The goods are delivered to the buyer, who signs the **delivery note** to show that the goods have been accepted. The buyer completes a **goods received note** to show that the goods have been received. The **sales invoice** shows the buyer how much to pay, when and how. The seller may then send the buyer a **receipt** to show that payment has been accepted.

Try this (page 71)

Sarah needs to include her personal details, the likely costs and revenues of the business, her market research, details of how and where she intends to set up, any other financial information (such as projections of profit and breakeven), her own contribution to the business in terms of both experience and investment, and the short- and long-term objectives of the business.

The balance sheet

Test yourself (page 73)

1 Cash in hand — asset	6 Furniture — asset
2 Cash in the bank — asset	7 Machinery — asset
3 Creditors — liability	8 Overdrafts — liability
4 Debtors — asset	9 Stock — asset
5 Factory — asset	10 Vehicles — asset

Try this (page 73)

(a) total assets in 2005 = fixed assets (£235,000) + current assets (£245,000) = £480,000

total assets in 2007 = fixed assets (£250,000) + current assets (£270,000) = £520,000

The increase is therefore £520,000 − £480,000 = £40,000.

(b) Fiveways Farm has added to its fixed assets, probably by buying new vehicles or machinery. It could also have invested in new technology, such as production or computer facilities to go with the new yoghurt production.

Profit and loss account

Test yourself (page 76)

Trading account		£000	£000
Sales revenue			20,000
minus Cost of sales			
	Opening stock	12,000	
	plus Purchases	5,500	
	minus Closing stock	2,000	**15,500**
Gross profit			**4,500**
minus Expenses	Rent	500	
	Wages	2,000	
	Transport	750	
	Power	500	
	Equipment	500	**4,250**
Net **profit**			**250**

The amount of **profit** is therefore **£250,000**.

Try this (page 76)

(a) Sarah's net profit margin can be calculated through (net profit/sales revenue) × 100 or (300/21,000) × 100 = 1.42%. This means that she is making just 1.4p on every pound of sales. This is not a very satisfactory level. Money banked at no risk would make more than this (as long as interest rates were higher than 1.4%).

Sarah's gross profit margin = (gross profit/sales revenue) × 100 or (5,000/21,000) × 100 = 23.8% or 23.8p on every pound of sales. This is healthy.

(b) Sarah is carrying too much stock: she has only sold a net amount of £2,500 worth but has still bought extra stock worth £5,500. Had she not bought this stock, her gross profit would have been £10,500 and her net profit £5,800. The difference between Sarah's net and gross profits also shows that her expenses are too high. This means that she needs to look at her level of expenses to improve the net position. In particular, Sarah appears to be paying too high a rent on her premises and possibly too much in wages, so she should look at ways to reduce these.

Cash and cash flow

Test yourself (page 79)

For the examples given:
- Sole trader inflows are likely to be limited to revenue from sales. Outflows will include payments for stock, rent or mortgage on premises, heating and lighting, and wages for any staff.
- For the manufacturing company, inflows are again likely to be limited to revenue from sales of goods, although they may also come from supplying services. Outflows will include stock, cost of premises, components and materials, power, wages, vehicles and maintenance.
- For the supermarket it is likely that part of the inflows are rents (from other businesses taking space in stores) plus car park fees and charges on store and credit cards. The main inflow will still be sales revenue. Outflows will include stock, power, advertising and marketing, wages, bonuses and theft from stores.

Try this (page 79)

In November, Schwitt had cash in (revenue) of £80,000 but total payments of £95,000, giving it a negative cash flow. October also had a negative cash flow (−£15,000) and this resulted in an overdraft, which November's position has increased. If this trend continues, the company will have cash-flow difficulties. It can be seen that the forecast sales increase for December will solve these, so Schwitt is relying on good sales at this time of year. However, it is also forecast that payments will increase, particularly advertising expenditure, so this trend needs to be monitored. The company is probably relying too heavily on December sales and needs to look at cutting back on some of its expenses.

Understanding and using ratios

Test yourself (page 83)

Check your answer against the definitions on page 82.

Try this (page 83)

(a) 'Expenses' could include rent, wages and equipment.

(b) Profitability ratios measure how much profit the business is making compared with revenue. In 2006, Merrion's made £15,000 gross profit on £30,000 of sales revenue, a ratio of 15,000:30,000 or 1:2 or (£15,000/£30,000) × 100 = 50% profit margin, or £5 gross profit for every £10 of sales. In 2007, sales revenue and gross profit increased, but the business was not actually as profitable as before. In 2007, Merrion's made £18,000 gross profit on £40,000 of sales revenue, a ratio of $(18,000/40,000) \times 100 = 45\%$ profit margin, or £4.50 gross profit for every £10 of sales.

However, Merrion's would look at net profit as the more important figure to see if the business had improved financially. There is increased production and sales, but also increased costs, so the comparison of ratios is important. Net profit to sales (2006) was $(£5,000/£30,000) \times 100 = 16.6\%$. In 2007, this was $(£7,000/£40,000) \times 100 = 17.5\%$, so profitability increased, but only just.

Test on Chapter 4 (page 83)

1 C	2 A	3 E	4 C	5 D
6 E	7 D	8 B	9 B	10 D
11 C	12 C	13 A	14 D	15 D

Chapter 5

Pay and benefits

Test yourself (page 87)

| 1 F | 2 A | 3 D | 4 E | 5 C | 6 G | 7 B |

Try this (page 88)

Time rate is where a worker is paid for the amount of time he or she spends in doing a job — usually 'per hour'. Piece rate is payment for the number of pieces produced or jobs done. This change is likely to benefit the business, as the team will be keen to wash and valet as many cars as possible. However, it could also lead to the job being rushed and therefore lower quality. It could benefit the team members, as they can earn more money by dealing with more cars.

Recruitment

Test yourself (page 90)

Human resources writes a **job description** to show what tasks, skills and qualifications are needed and a **person specification** to show the sort of worker that will fit the requirements. It **advertises** the post and invites **applications**. Using letters and **CVs** that are sent in, it draws up a **short list** of the **applicants** it thinks are best qualified.

These become **candidates** and are invited to **interview**. The successful **interviewee** is offered the job.

Try this (page 90)

(a) A person specification is used to outline details of the type of person whom the business needs to recruit.

(b) Sarah needs someone with particular skills and qualifications. The skills required are people skills (working directly with customers) and specialist hairdressing skills and qualifications. Sarah might decide that she wants someone with experience or someone whom she can train up herself, and she would need to make this clear in the specification.

The details are important so that Sarah has a good idea of exactly the sort of person she wants, and can match applicants to these details.

Training, development and appraisal

Test yourself (page 92)

| 1 B | 2 E | 3 C | 4 E | 5 D |

Try this (page 93)

(a) Induction training is the training given to new staff as an introduction to a business.

(b) The new employees will need to know about various aspects of the workplace. They will need to:
- be introduced to other staff and to the methods of working in the hairdresser's
- be given personal information, such as the location of cloakrooms and washroom facilities
- learn about health and safety, particularly with regard to electrical apparatus and water in hairdresser's; a list of 'dos and don'ts' would be useful
- be told about fire drill procedures
- know what Sarah regards as acceptable in terms of taking breaks, making telephone calls, holding personal conversations etc.

Rights and responsibilities at work

Test yourself (page 96)

| 1 E | 2 A | 3 C | 4 B | 5 D |

Try this (page 96)

As the jobs being done by the two people are similar,

they should be receiving similar pay. Rob may be entitled to slightly more if the business takes into account the expense of working in London, but this should not amount to twice the salary level.

According to the 1970 Equal Pay Act, men and women should receive equal pay for equal work. Judith's situation might also be illegal under the 1975 Sex Discrimination Act.

Judith should talk to her union representative or line manager. If the complaint cannot be solved by the management at the business, it may be necessary for her to take the case to an industrial tribunal.

Note There are no marks for quoting Acts or dates correctly — a description is sufficient.

Industrial relations

Test yourself (page 98)

Check your answers against the key points on page 97.

Try this   (page 98)

Employees could operate as a group to make sure that their pay is at the level being offered by the rest of the industry. If it isn't, they could use collective bargaining with Fiveways to ensure that it is in future.

Employees could act to make sure that their working conditions are as good as, or better than, other workers in the industry. Again, they could use collective bargaining, or could take industrial action to improve working conditions if they felt that this was justified. A trade union would provide them with expert advice and help in any negotiations. It might also support them if they took industrial action.

Motivation

Test yourself (page 100)

Check your answer against the diagram on page 99.

Try this   (page 101)

One way of using money would be for Sarah to introduce bonuses for the staff. These could, for example, be linked to customer comment cards so that the staff member who got the most favourable comments received the bonus. All staff could be rewarded with bonuses if a certain number of customers were attracted. This would encourage staff to recommend the hairdresser's. Bonuses could therefore bring benefits in increased revenue or customer satisfaction.

The cheapest way to motivate staff without using money is the use of praise. This makes the staff feel better and work harder. Sarah could also introduce perks like free haircuts or other extras.

Test on Chapter 5   (page 101)

From the point of view of the employee, extra skills are being gained that may make them worth more in the labour market and able to move on to better-paid jobs. Such training may make them more motivated to succeed. On the down side, workers may feel that such training is unnecessary, if they cannot see an immediate use for it. Older workers, in particular, may resent having to go through training programmes if they cannot see any benefit to themselves.

From the point of view of the business, a labour force that is better qualified may be more likely to leave. This would be a bad thing, as the business will have paid for the training, but another business will then be benefiting from this investment. On the plus side, training means that workers are a lot more flexible, and a better-trained workforce should produce better-quality goods and higher sales. Training also provides the business with a pool of labour that might be useful at some time in the future.

Note Where possible, you should use the case study to back your argument. For example, it would be useful to the business to have staff with management and language skills in its overseas operations. To reach the higher marks, your conclusion must be based on the analysis and reasons that you have given.

Chapter 6

Chain of production

Test yourself (page 105)

Check your answers against the definitions and diagrams on pages 102–104.

Try this   (page 105)

(a) The tertiary sector is the third part of the process of production (after primary and secondary) and refers to services. Retailers and plumbers are examples.

(b) Businesses can achieve this either by being physically close to customers — many tertiary businesses are located in town centres or other populated areas

— or by going to customers (plumbers, electricians and other tradespersons, for example). One way to achieve this is to be easily contactable or to provide additional services (such as booking a car service via telephone or the internet).

Methods of production

Test yourself (page 108)

1 C   2 D   3 B   4 C   5 A

Try this   (page 108)

The benefits are that each of the three people named should be able to develop expertise in their own area. They should be able to concentrate on their own job and not have to worry about anyone else's — they will therefore become more efficient at their tasks.

The drawbacks are the difficulties that might arise if one of the three falls ill or leaves the business. For example, Jeb could go off to college or to get married. If this happened, his expertise would be lost to the farm and Dan would have to buy it in from elsewhere. Second, any of the three could become bored with just doing one job and this could lead to a lack of motivation and efficiency.

Management of quality

Test yourself (page 111)

Check your answers against the key terms on page 109.

Try this   (page 111)

TQM means that everyone is responsible for quality, including those businesses responsible for the inputs to the process, such as raw materials. By encouraging workers to be involved, faults and problems will be spotted earlier. The responsibility given to workers may also help to motivate them. The earlier a fault is spotted, the sooner it can be put right and the less production is lost. If production were only checked once complete, a whole production run could be wasted as it is unlikely that any inputs could be recovered.

Business location

Test yourself (page 113)

The production process takes goods from **raw materials** to **finished product**. Sometimes this involves a decrease in volume, sometimes an increase. A **bulk-increasing** industry is one where the product becomes harder to transport as it passes through the process. An example

is **wood** being turned into **furniture** (or any similar example). A **bulk-decreasing** industry is one where the product becomes easier to transport as it passes through the process. An example is **apples** being turned into **apple juice** (or any similar example). The business should locate where **transport costs** will be lowest.

Try this   (page 114)

(a) E-commerce means bringing buyers and sellers together via web/internet technology.

(b) Benefits include government grants and other possible concessions, such as reduced taxation and business rates. There is also likely to be a good pool of available labour. Disadvantages are the distance from the current base and the costs of setting up, including the costs of training new staff.

Note Top marks are earned for presenting a balanced view, outlining both the advantages of an Enterprise Zone and the disadvantages of a new location at a distance from the current one.

Test on Chapter 6 (page 114)

(a) It is a good idea because Merrion's wants to be able to offer its customers quality products and services. This will ensure customer loyalty and help the business. If products are not of the required quality, this would cause extra costs to the businesses either through customers returning products or through the business having to return products to suppliers.

(b) Merrion's could ensure that its suppliers are all part of a quality scheme such as ISO 9001 or a similar quality mark. It could make sure that it builds up a good relationship with suppliers so they are aware of the quality that is required and acceptable. This may also involve providing suppliers with training. Merrion's could introduce financial penalties for suppliers that do not meet its standards. Ultimately, it could stop using these suppliers and concentrate only on those who can supply quality items.

Chapter 7

Market research

Test yourself (page 118)

Check your answers against the key points on page 117.

Try this (page 118)

(a) SWOT analysis is a research tool used by a business to identify internal Strengths and Weaknesses of a business (which can be influenced by the business) and external Opportunities and Threats to a business (which cannot be influenced by the business). (*Note* You must mention 'external' and 'internal' to gain full marks.)

(b) The owners need to build on their strengths. They could, for example, make sure that the new competition is not too much of a threat by moving into other products and different markets. They could also make sure that they offer a really good service to their existing customers in order to keep their loyalty. (*Note* The marks here are for reasoning and judgement, rather than for any particular choices.)

Product

Test yourself (page 121)

1 E   2 A   3 B   4 D   5 C

Try this (page 121)

Product diversification is when a business produces different types of product that allow it to move into other markets. The purpose of diversification is to spread risks and increase revenue across different markets.

Products might be variations on those the business already sells, so for Dan they could be dairy-based products such as flavoured yoghurts or different cheeses, or they could be different products altogether — for example, Dan might want to open a farm shop.

Product life cycles

Test yourself (page 124)

Check your answers against the diagram and definitions on page 122.

Try this (page 125)

The sales of caged birds have fallen over recent years. This has been accompanied by a fall in the sales of bird food and other products, leading to a fall in revenue. The sales of cages will thus also have fallen and the market for this product has shrunk. It is likely that the market is nearing the end of its product life cycle. The business should look for evidence of where customers who used to keep caged birds now spend their income and consider introducing products in a growth area such

as this. (*Note* You must refer to as much of the data as possible.)

Price

Test yourself (page 127)

1 C   2 F   3 E   4 A   5 D   6 B

Try this (page 127)

The marks here will be awarded for the strength of your arguments rather than your decision. Possible points to make are outlined below. If Sarah charged lower prices:
- she might attract more customers than her competitors
- she might not cover her costs or make a profit
- people might think that the quality of her haircuts was poor
- competitors might also lower prices and force Sarah out of business

If she charged higher prices:
- she might not attract enough customers
- she might make more profit
- she might target a particular market that thinks she is providing a quality product

Promotion

Test yourself (page 130)

Promotion is the way a business **informs** customers about products and **persuades** them to buy. Advertising is **publicity** for a product that is paid for directly; it is therefore called **above-the-line** expenditure. Advertising is used to **promote** products through broadcast and print **media**. Advertising that is not directly paid for is called **below-the-line** expenditure. This includes **promotions** such as money-off coupons and special offers.

Try this (page 130)

No marks will usually be awarded for your choice. The marks are given for the reasons that you provide to back your choice. Here are some examples:
- 'Three for the price of two' offers will encourage customers to buy more products, give them greater value for money and make them more loyal. However, it could prove costly and reduce profits.
- Selling other products, such as cat and dog flaps and bird cages, could appeal to a wider market and bring in new customers, who then may also buy from the original product range. However, some of these products may be bulky and expensive to deliver.

- Providing a 'satisfaction or your money back' guarantee might increase customer value and loyalty, but could prove expensive if goods were not of a sufficiently high standard.
- Providing a monthly newsletter to customers would increase customer value, help keep customers loyal and act as a way of promoting particular products. However, it could be expensive to produce and distribute.

Place (distribution)

Test yourself (page 133)

Check your answers against the key terms on page 132.

Try this (page 133)

There will usually be no marks given for making the choice. The marks are awarded for the reasons that you give to back up your choice. You should use the ideas supplied. For example, 'aiming global' might have the following consequences:
- Increased profits are likely from increased sales.
- Distribution costs will rise — this could outweigh any increased profit.
- New technology could cost more than the increased profit.
- Staying local could help to keep costs down and help it to keep its specialist market.

Test on Chapter 7 (page 134)

1 C	2 C	3 C	4 C	5 D
6 C	7 D	8 B	9 C	10 B

Chapter 8

Customer service

Test yourself (page 138)

Information	■ accurate ■ helpful ■ clear
Advice	■ specialist ■ as required
After-sales	■ delivery ■ packaging ■ warranties
Ways to pay	■ cash ■ credit/debit cards

Try this (page 138)

Information may be given in any of the following ways: directly by staff via the telephone, mail or through an email response service; on websites and in other published material such as mail order catalogues and price lists; on the packaging or other information that comes with the product; on invoices, bills or accounts sent out to customers; on publicity materials such as newspaper advertisements and leaflets.

Some information, such as ingredients, has to be provided by law. In other cases, it is provided to help customers.

Measuring customer satisfaction

Test yourself (page 140)

Check your answers against the diagram on page 139.

Try this (page 140)

Market research gives information about customers and potential customers. This can be used to improve each part of the marketing mix. Advertisements and other promotions can be targeted at these groups; products can be altered to appeal to certain groups; prices can be changed to reflect what customers are willing to pay. Market research also helps the business to plan for the future. In terms of customer satisfaction, information and advice can be provided and this can be changed to fit customer expectations. Customer satisfaction can be measured — for instance, by looking at how many customers return for future purchases or return goods to stores — and changes made to improve it.

Consumer protection

Test yourself (page 143)

1 D	2 C	3 C	4 A	5 D

Try this (page 143)

The Latin tag 'caveat emptor' means 'let the buyer beware'. It is important because it means that, in consumer law, the first thing that must happen is for consumers to behave sensibly. Consumers are expected to take care to make sure that they have bought the right product for the purpose and that they have read, understood and followed any instructions. In this case, as Sarah did not advise the customer, it is the customer's own fault that she bought the wrong colour. It is therefore not Sarah's responsibility to do anything about compensating the customer. The advice to Sarah could be to ignore the customer. Better advice might be to explain the situation but perhaps give the customer some benefit to keep her happy — a reduced price product or service for example — as this would be better customer service.

Test on Chapter 8 (page 144)

1 D	2 C	3 B	4 C	5 C
6 C	7 A	8 A	9 A	10 B

Chapter 9
E-commerce and the internet

Test yourself (page 148)

Check your answers against the key terms on page 146.

Try this (page 148)

Problems for the business include: customer reluctance to use computers, particularly if this means entering sensitive information such as bank account details; the costs and organisation required for delivery; the costs and expertise needed to set up a website and associated systems; ongoing maintenance and updating costs.

Problems for customers include: security issues; the fact that not all customers will have a computer or internet access; possible difficulties in returning unwanted goods.

The European Union

Test yourself (page 150)

Check your answers against the definitions on page 149.

Try this (page 151)

Harmonisation means bringing something into agreement with something else. In the EU, it means making sure that everyone uses the same weights and measures, and sometimes even laws.

This makes it easier for UK businesses to trade in Europe, as they do not have to convert sizes, amounts, distances etc. It also means that UK businesses can compete on the same level with other EU businesses if all face the same laws, taxes and restrictions. For Fiveways, it means that it can sell yoghurts in standard sizes and packaging throughout its markets and is subject to the same laws and restrictions as its European competitors.

The euro enables all the countries of the EU to trade in the same currency. Even though the UK did not convert to the euro, UK businesses can still trade in this currency, making it easier to do business in Europe.

International trade and globalisation

Test yourself (page 153)

1 A	2 D	3 B	4 B	5 C

Try this (page 154)

At the exchange rate given, each car would cost €10,000 or, in sterling, £7,000. The garage should therefore accept the euro price. The reason this price is lower is because the German business would have no currency conversion charges; nor would it be subject to changes in exchange rates if it accepted a euro price.

Fair trade

Test yourself (page 156)

1 C	2 A	3 D	4 B

Try this (page 156)

(a) Emerging nations should benefit from more employment and by getting fairer prices for the goods they produce. This should raise their living standards. The disadvantage to emerging nations is that they may have to change domestic laws and practices to fit in with the rest of the world. This can be expensive and culturally damaging. The expansion in trade may also damage the environment.

(b) Established trading nations gain a good reputation, but this is of little use unless fair trade also brings increased profits. They may cause damage to their own industries by letting them compete openly.

Test on Chapter 9 (page 156)

(a) Ethical constraints are those restrictions or drawbacks that society imposes on a business. They are based on what society thinks is 'right' or 'wrong'.

(b) In the case of Royaume, its advertising should, first, be neither illegal nor offensive. The business should not make false claims for the products or use images or words to which people might take offence. This includes rude, offensive or religious images. The image to which Muslims took offence should be removed and changed for one that is not offensive. This should also have been checked before the image was used.

Royaume should not claim that Zipfast shoes can help you run or recover faster unless there is scientific evidence to prove this. If there are, for instance, athletes who are happy to endorse the product, and say that it has had this effect on them, this would be allowed as an opinion, but to state such claims as fact is misleading, so they should be withdrawn.

(c) Royaume may be unethical in making claims for its products that it cannot prove. It would be unethical for it to use religious symbols to promote products, but in this case, it looks like a mistake rather than a deliberate attempt to do so.